HERE THERE BE MONSTERS

A Terrifying True Story of Abuse, Endurance, and Hope in Small Town America

David Leroy Harter Finch

Here There Be Monsters
Copyright © 2023 David Leroy Harter Finch

Produced and printed by Stillwater River Publications.
All rights reserved. Written and produced in the
United States of America. This book may not be reproduced
or sold in any form without the expressed, written
permission of the author and publisher.

Visit our website at
www.StillwaterPress.com
for more information.

First Stillwater River Publications Edition

ISBN: 978-1-960505-19-4

Library of Congress Control Number: 2023904958

1 2 3 4 5 6 7 8 9 10
Written by David Leroy Harter Finch.
Cover illustration and interior design by Elisha Gillette.
Published by Stillwater River Publications,
Pawtucket, RI, USA.

*The views and opinions expressed
in this book are solely those of the author
and do not necessarily reflect the views
and opinions of the publisher.*

To all the survivors.

This book details the author's experience with child abuse, sexual assault, and domestic violence. Please be warned.

HERE THERE BE MONSTERS

TABLE OF CONTENTS

Foreword	xi
The Rise of the House of Usher	1
A Life Before	11
A Sleepy Little Town	15
Childhood Lost	25
The Players	27
Paint Chips	45
Food as a Weapon	51
Memories of the Color Red	57
Together, Alone	65
Clothes Are a Privilege	71
School Days	77
Playing Charades	83
The Long Cold Walk	89
My Brother's Keeper	93
Behind the Cellar Door	99
Comfortably Numb	109
Bricks and Crosses	113
Three Sheets in Three Minutes	117
Wait Until Your Father Gets Home	123
The Bad Hat	127
My Summer in the Shithouse with Pete Rose on a Bed of Nails	135
Same Song, Different Verse	139
Cinderella Stories	147
Not in the Face	155
The Final Straw	163
The Danger of Hope	167
My Day in Court	179
On Living Life as A Survivor	189
In the Darkness, I Dreamed	203
Let Me Vent for a Bit Here	209
Family	211
Final Thoughts	219
Postscript	225
Afterword	229
About the Author	233

FOREWORD

My name is Lisa Ann Harter Pettit, and David is my younger brother.

My brother was such a cute young child, with blond hair and blue eyes. He was always curious and loved to play sports and games. And he was always sweet—a really good kid.

In this book, David has written a true account of what happened during his childhood. I know his recollections are true because I was a witness, and I also suffered horrific abuse.

I feel it's important for you to read this book. I want people to know the truth behind the perfect façade of our beautiful house and perfect parents.

I hope this book will help people take a closer look if they suspect child abuse, and hopefully that will save children from the hell that we lived through.

— 1 —

THE RISE OF THE HOUSE OF USHER

Everyone has a dream home. You know the kind I'm talking about. It's one of those big, two-bedroom places with lots of windows and a white picket fence. It's the perfect place to raise your two-point-five kids and park your blue minivan—the ultimate American family home. Different houses appeal to different people's tastes, of course, and no two dream homes are ever the same. Yet, it seems to me, everyone has one.

For my stepmother Lucille, her dream house was an old colonial fixer-upper. She hated the house we lived in on Myra Road; it was perfectly fine, just too modern for her taste. But more important than that, she hated the memories of my birth mother that still lingered there. Shades of my birth mother's life haunted my father, too. Little reminders of her were everywhere, such as in a picture on the wall, a knickknack, or a random, even unimportant piece of furniture in the living room. All of these tiny echoes of her life were a constant reminder to my father—sad and painful ghosts of a wife and son he had lost so tragically.

With these factors in mind, Lucille set about on a campaign to find the house of her dreams to escape my father's heartbreaking past. A "new" old house was required to make a fresh start, a place to create her own new, unique family memories. Lucille had always been fascinated by antiques; she had acquired many, and insisted upon a period-appropriate house to display them in. It needed to be a vintage house that would complement her treasured antique collection ever-so-perfectly. Her dream was to create a literal museum to showcase her tastefully acquired collection to anyone who cared to ask. That was the kind of house she was looking for. It would be her ultimate dream home. And she spent several years seeking this ideal old house to make her very own, personal fairytale come true.

House hunting can be a practice in futility at times, but my stepmother Lucille was relentless and never gave up her search. Lucille would drag the entire family along with her on these frequent house hunting expeditions. She would often try to make a family day out of it, bringing along a lunch and blankets for us to spread out on. We would set up our picnic in an open field to eat, all the while fighting off the inevitable ant or mosquito invasions. After lunch, we would toss a Frisbee back and forth and chase dandelion fluff on the wind. I was so little then. These outings were adventurous times for me—exciting and happy days in the sun with family. We got the chance to visit and explore so many old places from those magical, mystical "olden times."

Most of the houses we looked at were, in fact, very old, but also had been restored and upgraded to modern codes and conveniences. This would simply not do. None of them fit Lucille's absolute requirement of a colonial fixer-upper—her perfect dream house. So, she kept looking...and looking...and *looking* for that one perfect house that would kill the ghosts and fulfill all her desires.

After a long string of these time-consuming, fruitless searches, Lucille came home one day very excited. She told my father that she had found the perfect house for us to buy and move into. Lucille and my father immediately went on a drive to see the house she had discovered. The rest was, as they say, history. They wasted no time and purchased Lucille's perfect new fixer-upper almost on the spot. Needless to say, Lucille was ecstatic.

I was excited too, but far too young to understand the implications of all that was happening around me. As soon as we moved in, I realized I had been taken away from all my friends. I didn't realize it then, of course, but I had also said goodbye to all that I had ever known to be a sane, comfortable family life.

When we moved into Lucille's dream house, so much changed right away. Notice I use the word "house" here, and not "home." I make this word choice quite intentionally. It was never "home" when I lived in that house. A home is a place where you are supposed to feel safe and sheltered from all the trouble in the world, but I never once felt safe there. I was never allowed to have a feeling of familial comfort or support of any kind. As the days, weeks, and months passed, that house became the ultimate symbol of fear, pain, and unthinkable abuse. Known locally as the historic Kitt's Tavern, it was only one town away from where I lived and played joyously for the first seven years of my life. It was only a few miles away, yet it felt worlds apart—worlds apart from the generous portions of comfort we had come to know at the house on Myra Road. Gone were the days of neighborhood friends. Also gone, for me, was the sanctity of the word "home" itself. The day after we moved into that house, my world began to spiral into a living nightmare.

When we first moved into Kitt's Tavern, it was in absolute ruins—and that's being kind. Shingles were missing in many places, leaving gaps on the sides of the house like the teeth in a Jack-O'-lantern's smile. The roof had multiple bare patches where shingles had blown off, exposing the ancient wood beneath. A fire had burned a portion of the front of the house and porch sometime years earlier. Little to nothing had been done to repair the damage after that. The house had not been lived in for years, assuming you don't count the rats, bats, birds, and mice. It had not been maintained at all. The house we moved

Kitt's Tavern today

into looked nothing like the gorgeous historical landmark it had once been, or that which it has been restored to today. What it did look like, to my young eyes anyway, was an old-fashioned haunted house. In fact, it appeared to have jumped right off the set of a horror film. *So, we are going to live here? Oh, joy!*

Inside the house, things were no better. In fact, they were much worse. The place was filthy. Years of rotting leaves, rodent feces, and dirt had accumulated and layered the floors. Cobwebs both old and new hung like tapestry around us, encased with dust from decades of neglect. The walls were in horrible shape as well. The plaster was stained and seemed to be collapsing in no matter where you looked. On the sections where the plaster had not already fallen off the wall, you could see remnants of the old, decrepit paint. On those spots where paint still remained, it was peeling off in big chips from the mildew caked and growing beneath it. The few paneled walls that were still standing had been wallpapered over long ago. Much of the remaining wallpaper hung from the walls in tattered strips. You could easily see rainwater damage, too. Rust-colored water stains streaked across everything, leaving little patches and trails of mold and decay. Even to my innocent, seven-year-old eyes, I knew this was not a good place to live in.

Through the cracks in the wall of the room I shared with my stepbrother Michael, I could see the outside world. We would watch the cars and trucks zip by on nearby Route 95 through those gaps while perched in our beds. We were able to see things this way until our father got to work and layered on some tarpaper, then re-shingled the house exterior. But until he put up that tarpaper, the wind and rain blew right into our bedroom with abandon.

At night, we would sleep cocooned in the relative safety of our blankets. Lucille tried to make it all seem exciting, somehow. We were camping out in our new house! It was all just one big, fun adventure! She believed we should be enjoying ourselves in our wonderful, new house. Remember, I was just a little kid at the time and I still had a lot to learn about the world. But I was disillusioned about that house right from the start. I may not yet have heard the saying that you can't polish a turd, but that saying applied to the condition of Kitt's Tavern when we first moved in. Looking at pictures of that house today, it would seem that I was wrong in my initial assessment. But I had no idea the depths that Lucille would go to fix up her dream house, or what the personal cost to me and my sister Lisa would be.

Kitt's Tavern, back then, was a great place to inspire childhood nightmares—it still inspires my nightmares to this day. The cellar terrified me. It was a dank, dark, and dusty place, and it was enormous. Rough, unfinished rock made up three of the walls, and it was all joined together by crumbling mortar. The front side of the cellar had two windows that faced the road but did little to light up the massive space. Eerie shadows danced on the walls and played tricks on my youthful eyes. The shifting light would constantly coalesce into phantom faces on the rocks and lines of mortar along the walls, and it terrified me. This cellar had so many corners to be afraid of, harboring a multitude of nooks and crannies. There were so many hiding places for nightmares to lurk, all waiting to jump out at an unsuspecting child when he least expected it.

The attic scared the living hell out of me, too. The chimney came right out of the middle of the floor, taking up a large square in the center of this huge room. An entire tree had been used as the main support for the roof and it was still in place. There was a small window at each end of the attic that never seemed to cast enough light to dispel its own disturbing shadows, even on the brightest day. The chimney's location, in the very center of the space, always left a part of the attic blocked from sight. That was the truly frightening part for me, not knowing what was on the other side, lurking in the seemingly unending blackness. It was so dark that it allowed my mind to manufacture the vilest of demons. I knew they were there. Just around the corner. Waiting. For me.

As for the rest of the house, there were other oddities as well—many of them spooky little features that you might find in any old house. For example, there were several hidey-holes on the second floor. One strange, tiny door in the bathroom led to a space under the attic stairs. Another door was hidden in the back of my closet and led to a hiding place alongside the massive chimney. It is no wonder I despised that house from day one and I have never changed my mind about that. I recall reading a short story by Edgar Allen Poe in college, "The Fall of the House of Usher." The opening paragraph of that story tells it all, and expresses exactly how I felt about that place, all summed up in the words of the immortal Mr. Poe:

> "...I know not how it was — but, with the first glimpse of the building, a sense of insufferable gloom pervaded my spirit. I say insufferable; for the feeling was unrelieved by any of that half-pleasurable, because poetic, sentiment, with which the mind usually receives even the sternest natural images of the desolate or terrible. I looked upon the scene before me — upon the mere house, and the simple

landscape features of the domain — upon the bleak walls — upon the vacant eye-like windows — upon a few rank sedges — and upon a few white trunks of decayed trees — with an utter depression of soul which I can compare to no earthly sensation more properly than to the after-dream of the reveler upon opium — the bitter lapse into every-day life — the hideous dropping off of the veil. There was an iciness, a sinking, a sickening of the heart — an unredeemed dreariness of thought which no goading of the imagination could torture into aught of the sublime. What was it — I paused to think — what was it that so unnerved me in the contemplation of the House of Usher?"

―――

    I am eight years old and I am locked in the attic. Again. I am terrified of the attic, but my mommy scares me more. She knows I am terrified of the attic, that is why she locked me up here in the first place. I am being punished for a horribly negligent act—I failed to dust the rocking chair in the kitchen well enough. I only missed a tiny spot, but that spot is enough to bring out the monster inside her. She gets so angry at me that she drags me up the stairs to the second floor by my hair and my earlobe. As we stand at the door to the attic, she unlocks it. Then she turns around and looks me up and down, gauging my fear. I am unable to hide it. Then her face breaks into that smirk I have come to know so well, and to fear so very much. She orders me to go into the attic and stay there until she thinks I am sorry enough. She then reaches up and pulls the string to turn off the light. With that simple act, she acknowledges my fear of the dark. She shuts and locks the attic door leaving me alone in the dimly lit attic with no one for company but my terror. I want to turn the light back on, but I know mommy will be watching. The thought of being caught with the light on turns my bowels to water. I am terrified.
    There are shadows everywhere. Behind every box, in every corner, there is a monster lurking there that wants to eat me. I am certain of

that fact, but I also know that if I don't move, the monster won't be able see me. I huddle down in between two boxes, covering myself with a blanket I find to make myself as small as I can. I hide there, shaking. My teeth are chattering. I start to cry, alone in the creeping darkness of the attic. My ear still hurts from being pulled on so hard, but that pain takes a backseat to my terror. I hear my mommy call my brother and sisters for lunch, but there will be no lunch for me. I know that I am banished. Now I have to go pee, but I am afraid to call out to ask permission to use the bathroom. If I call out, the monsters will hear me. All of them.

I have now wet myself. I am ashamed. My tears continue to dribble down my face. I have been up here for so long. It seems like it has been hours. It must have been hours. I start to doze off, but I jolt awake. Somehow, I had nodded off here in my hiding place. When I realize I am still in the attic and it was not just a dream, I start to shake and cry once again, I cannot stop. Why has my mommy done this to me? Suddenly I hear the lock being turned on the attic door. The door opens and the light is switched back on. The blessed light banishes the shadows and makes the monsters run away. Mommy comes up the stairs and asks me if I am sorry for what I did. I wholeheartedly tell her that yes, I am very sorry. I swear to her it will never happen again. She smirks that hateful smirk at me and tells me to go downstairs to join the family for supper. I can't believe she made me spend the entire day up here, left alone in my own, private little hell. Am I that bad of a child? I do not understand why my mommy treats me so.

I will try harder. I will do anything to make her love me.

Over time, the interior of the house became more livable, due to a lot of our father's hard work and old-fashioned elbow grease. He tore the hardwood floors out of the attic and reused them to replace the worn floors in the kitchen. All the glass panes in the many windows in the house had to be replaced and reglazed. It was an exciting time to be a young boy with all this construction activity going on. Watching my father tear down all that horsehair plaster and wooden slats that lay beneath them was amazing. Then he would mix new plaster and install new ceilings. I loved to watch him work. I was so proud. He was my father, and he could do anything!

As he worked, I discovered my specialty was getting in the way, just like most little boys tend to do. I got a lot of splinters, stepped on a few nails, and made a general nuisance of myself trying to help where help was not wanted nor needed.

Very shortly, I would rue the day I innocently offered to help. Someone inside the house saw me and decided I might be of use. Someone saw a purpose for my existence at last, and my carefree days were destined to vanish quickly under a mountain of forced labor. In my mother's eyes, I could become a valuable tool after all.

When I moved to Kitt's Tavern, I was just seven years old and happy. But by the time I turned nine, my life had shifted cruelly to be off-kilter, and feelings of happiness had become just a distant memory. Although I was young, I was aware something was not right; I had no friends, nor was I allowed any. I had no free time or playtime anymore. All the free time I did have was swallowed up whole by Lucille's infinite list of chores. Kitt's Tavern could have and should have been a wonderful place to grow up in, but that was not to be.

It turned out that my first impression of Kitt's Tavern had been sadly prophetic. When we pulled into the driveway that fateful day, everything in my world changed. There was no more joy in my life; it was to be sucked dry by the needs of that damned house and the obsessions of my stepmother, Lucille. I learned many lessons in that house back then, but I learned of the existence of monsters most of all. Yes, they are real.

— 2 —

A LIFE BEFORE

In contrast, I do have some very fond memories of living in our small house on Myra Road. Many of these recollections are centered around the Christmas holiday.

Christmas was a wonderful time to be alive in the house of my early childhood. It was a small, three-bedroom ranch with a finished basement. There was even an added room in the basement that my oldest sister, Lori, used as her bedroom. The house was well taken care of, clean, and well decorated. It was a wonderful place to be a kid. My father had the garage knocked down and replaced it with an extended living room with a fireplace. It was in this extended living room where we had our Christmas tree and opened all our presents. The tree was always a real blue spruce, too. An artificial tree was never a consideration in our house. (Fake trees were just too tacky.) I still do love the smell of a blue spruce tree. It will always smell like Christmas, to me.

In the weeks leading up to the holiday, I would get to go over Meme and Pepe's house where I would "help" make massive numbers of Christmas cookies with Meme. She would let me spread some of the frosting onto the sugar cookie candy canes, trees, and reindeer. I loved those days because they were so much fun. I would watch Meme as she expertly baked all those wonderful Christmas treats. I loved to watch her cook. I would wait, poised and ready to do the most important job in the kitchen, just for her: I would lick out all of the bowls and eat every last speck of batter on the mixer beaters. It was tough, getting off all that delicious frosting and batter, but I knew I was the best man for the job. I eventually came to realize, at some point, that licking the bowls and beaters was not a real job. But I did not care; it was quality time with Meme and, in that moment, I was her special little man.

At Myra Road, among all of the many Christmas decorations on display, there was an Advent calendar that hung on the basement door. I loved that calendar, too. You know the kind I am talking about—it was handcrafted out of wood and had little numbered doors that could be opened each day. We all got to take turns finding the number for the day and getting to open the door to see what picture it would reveal.

On our Christmas tree, we hung a golden, glitter-covered globe that could be split open to reveal a present inside. Each morning, on the days leading up to Christmas, one of us would be told that a special gift might be inside the magic ball having been left there just for us. The chosen one would run to the tree, open the magic ball, and find a secret gift just for them. The gifts it held were tiny—a toy car, a plastic ring, and the like. I remember how excited I was when it came around to be my turn. Decorations were everywhere in that house. Christmas carols played on the stereo. We would listen to Mario Lanza, Bing Crosby, and Jim Nabors belt out all the old holiday classics. This is what Christmas will always feel like to me. It is what it should be.

On the special morning, the tree would be surrounded by a massive pile of presents, all wrapped in festive paper and bows. Meme and Pepe would come over. As a family, my mother, my father, and all five of us kids would sit around the living room as the presents were passed out and opened. The sounds of tearing paper and exclamations of joy for a special present received would echo all around us. This, to me is what

Christmas morning is all about—just being happy with family. Everyone is smiling. Everyone is joyful. There were no shades of what was to come in my future; there was just the feeling of love from the family. A happy day of opening presents, good food, laughter, and music.

I remember so many good moments, like playing in the yard in the summer, chasing butterflies, and romping with some of the neighborhood kids. I remember watching my father mow and rake the lawn—my daddy could do anything. I recall a birthday party for my sister Lisa and me; flashes of cake and presents in the backyard are still burned into my memory. I remember sitting at the picnic table as our father gave my stepbrother, Michael, and me buzzcuts to help us deal with the summer heat, and laughing at the texture of the stubble his efforts left behind. I remember our German shepherd, Princess—before we had to get rid of her because of Michael's asthma, and how we all cried when she had to go. I remember watching the television in the basement and getting in trouble for watching horror films (Vincent Price was my hero). I remember listening to Dr. Suess stories while sitting on my father's lap, discovering my love of books. There were trips to the beach when I helped my father carry the cooler while walking gingerly on the hot sands. I remember my G.I. Joe action figure and the misery I put him through in our backyard sandbox. Then there was my big wheel tricycle, and all the time I spent tearing up and down the driveway in it. And I could never forget my first bike. It was red with training wheels, and my father taught me to ride it. I would put paper clips and playing cards in the spokes to make a wonderful clicking sound.

I loved life at Myra Road; I still remember that well. Yes, there were disturbing undertones brewing in the house that I did not understand yet, but my illusion of safety had not yet been shattered. I remember so many little things, fragments of memories, really. Most of all, I recall that I loved my father and, for some reason, that my stepmother frightened me at some primal level. But at least she never harmed me. Not there. Not yet.

At this period of my life, I still believed in Santa Claus. I still believed that my parents would always love me and keep me safe. Soon enough, both of those illusions would be torn asunder. But overall, those were happy days back at Myra Road. They soon became my measuring stick of what happiness was all about. In times to come, I would think back on those memories when happiness became so much harder—if not, impossible—to find. I am fortunate that I had these memories of Myra Road to withdraw back to in my mind. They became a tool in my survival. They existed in my secret happy place, where no monsters dared dwell.

— 3 —

A SLEEPY LITTLE TOWN

What can I say about Kitt's Tavern that could possibly make you understand the absolute dread I feel for that house? How can I make you comprehend the incapacitating fear I experience whenever my nightmares take me back within its walls?

The real-world Kitt's Tavern is located on a sharp bend on Weaver Hill Road in the sleepy little rural town of West Greenwich, Rhode Island. But as I've said, that old house has taken up a permanent address in my nightmares. The house itself is an absolute thing of beauty. It is an amazing, barn-red, two-story farmhouse that was built approximately thirty years before the American Revolutionary War. The structure is tucked neatly into the side of a hill and wrapped in well-tended gardens. An abundance of trees—perfect for climbing—grow in the back of the property, awaiting the next generation of children at play. A lush, green lawn encircles the entire house, the perfect place for a game of catch. A long dirt driveway plunges right through the middle of the property, making its way past a variety of quaint, restored outbuildings.

Kitt's Tavern is truly a sight to behold. So much painstaking restoration work has been done on it through the years that it has been brought back to its original splendor. By just looking at it, you feel as if a small slice of history has come to life in front of you.

Kitt's Tavern was constructed sometime around 1740 by Silas Matteson. Upon his death, the property was passed down to his son, Christopher—known as Kitt—who operated it as a tavern and a carriage house into the late 1700s. What little other information that I have been able to find suggests that the Matteson family owned the property into the 20th century. The house then fell into disrepair and was eventually owned by another prominent West Greenwich family until our family purchased it. Such an idyllic spot, so much history, so much beauty, so many haunting memories.

Houses like Kitt's Tavern often have colorful tales and urban legends associated with them, tales that have been passed down from generation to generation and have become intricately entwined in local lore. Some houses become known as murder houses, a place where a past violent act makes people see it as a sinister place. Other houses have had famous people live there, or, in the case of a carriage house like Kitt's Tavern, someone famous might have spent the night. Other houses are purportedly haunted by ghosts that go bump in the night, slam doors, and make the floorboards creak. Ghostly apparitions might flicker in the corner of your eye, but when you turn to look, they are gone. A house might have been a speakeasy during prohibition, or a house of ill repute. A house's reputation, based on its history, can change how people feel when they see it. It affects them. I wish that the walls could speak in the house of my youth. If they could, Kitt's Tavern's walls would tell a story of hell on earth for the children who once did dwell there. But alas, a house cannot put voice to what happened within it.

I have many fond memories of the sleepy little town of West Greenwich. When I think back upon those horrible days when I was a child, I smile sadly. I still think back on all of the could-have-beens, all the potential joy to be had in that town, and even today, I still grieve. I grieve for a happy childhood that never came to be. Yes, West Greenwich was a place of quiet beauty and good people and still remains so to this day. But to paraphrase the great bard, something was rotten in Denmark, and so many things were seen by townsfolk but never spoken of. The swamp-Yankee philosophy is to not get involved in other people's private affairs, so blind eyes always turned away. Small towns like to keep their secrets, but secrets tend to trickle out into the light every now and then. Every town has its bad apples, as sure as rain is wet; some people just love to see pain in other people's eyes. This is a sad but harsh truth that I learned all too well as a child.

What I remember most about West Greenwich was the overwhelming beauty of it all. The town was comprised of mostly two-lane, curving, hilly country roads that wound between the homes of its inhabitants. There were trees everywhere—countless trees, as far as the eye could see. As a child you could lose yourself out there in the woods for an entire day looking for adventure. Running around, turning over rocks and branches, looking for snakes and salamanders, or even worms for fishing. You could walk the woods happily grazing off wild blueberries, raspberries, and grapes. I remember the earthy smell of the woods, the smell of the pines, and the tangy taste of the fruit on my tongue. The memory of the princess pine as it gently brushed against my legs as I passed through, is still alive with me to this day. I found so much peace in those woods when I was allowed to be there. I would sit on the banks of Big River to watch the water and fish as they passed me by. I would walk down the many game trails to seek adventure, certain that I would find some hidden treasure out among the trees. I know now that treasure was there every time I walked those paths, I just did not see it. The treasure was the serenity I felt, the calm inner peace that the woods gifted to me every time I passed through them.

The changing of the seasons always brought out an explosion of colors in the leaves of those trees. The varied shades of green in the spring and summer all gently blew in the breeze. Then, in the fall, came the bright reds, the luminous oranges, and quiet yellows with the green of the pines mixed between them all. Eventually, when winter came, all you could see were the stark, gray, bare trees. Trees stood like vertical slashes against the pure white of the snow, in front of the only color in sight from the evergreens. Evergreens can live through anything and still flourish—after all the abuse Mother Nature could throw at them, they would still stand.

West Greenwich, like many other small, sleepy towns in America, might look dull and unexciting to an outsider. But to the locals, this was not the case. We had volunteer fire departments waiting for the ring of the telephone, always ready to jump into action when people were in need. There were no cell phones or pagers in those days; only the loud ringing of the bell on the desk phone was their call to arms. The firehouses were social hubs as well, a place to gather and be among friends. They were places to swap tall tales and listen to the old men talk about the good old days gone by.

Then there were the chowder and clam cake dinners that the firehouses sponsored to raise funds. I loved those dinners—all you can eat chowder and clam cakes is just a bit south of heaven, but damned close to paradise in my eyes. My Pepe would swing by and take all of the family, all of us—no one was excluded—to those chowder and clam cake feasts. The whole family would stand in line, gathered together, waiting, while Pepe would pay for us all and then find a table with enough room for us to sit together. I miss fresh chowder and clam cakes so badly these days, as they are not available where I now reside. But those days, those happy few days, were a slice of heaven to me—my personal nirvana. I ate, and ate, and ate, until I could eat no more. The chowder was so sweet; the milky broth with potatoes and clams was perfect, with just a dash of salt and pepper.

Now, I have to talk about the clam cakes—I have never tasted anything in my life that is equal to the flavor of hot clam cakes fresh out of the fryolator. Flour, buttermilk, and clams are the main ingredients. There are variations on the theme, of course, but the result is all the same. Small, tasty balls of deep-fried ambrosia. I might be overplaying my card here, I admit, but I really do love them and could see myself becoming addicted to them if given the chance. Those days were such good days, sitting back, napkin in lap, gorging on heaven. And all the while, Pepe would be complaining that the cooks had tied a clam to a string and dragged it through the chowder just to give it a little flavor. It was his favorite complaint, and I loved to hear him repeat it with a whole lot of colorful language thrown in.

But I did not personally get to experience everything West Greenwich was like as a youth and a teenager. It was not to be. For most of it, I was on the outside looking in, forced to live vicariously through others. I watched from the sidelines of this life, observing what life should be like. I watched others drink in all of the joy that there was to be had in that town. But for me, that well had gone dry a long time before, and I knew better than to try to take another sip.

A New England native, I was born with no choice but to be a Red Sox baseball fan. I would sit and watch the games on TV with my Pepe, in his lap or on the couch next to his recliner. God, I might have been maybe three or four years old at the time. Pepe would regale me with stories of the great Carl "The Yaz" Yastrzemski and his teammates, all the while yelling at the umpires for being blind. Any call that went against the Sox was a bad one, in Pepe's eyes. Because of this, I swear I thought all umpires were blind when I was young.

My father loved baseball as well. He grew up in a small town in Pennsylvania named after the legendary athlete, Jim Thorpe. My father played baseball and basketball in high school. I have seen the articles of his career in an old scrapbook he had stored in the attic. He had pitched two no-hitters in his senior year of high school, so he of course loved pitching and baseball. It was just natural that as soon as my brother and I became old enough, we would be standing in line for sign-ups in the parking lot of Metcalf Middle School to register for Little League. We were in the fourth grade, if I recall correctly, and I was as excited as a boy can get at that age.

(I am going to sidetrack a tiny bit here. This was when I first met Joan and Gil Tourgee, names that I know mean so much to so many boys from those years. Mr. and Mrs. Tourgee donated so much of their time to the kids from the towns of Exeter and West Greenwich, RI, and instilled the love of baseball in two generations of youth. They selflessly dealt with all of the logistics of running the leagues, the paperwork, the uniforms, equipment, and, at the end of the season, the banquet, making sure every child got a trophy. I know others helped, but sadly, I don't know who they were, so I cannot acknowledge them here.)

Okay, back to it. There were tryouts for the Little League teams and if you did not make it, you were assigned to the instructional farm league. My aspirations of becoming Yaz did not come to fruition that day. I was not good at all. In fact, I actually stunk at the game. But I did get to play ball, and it was fun.

Little League was essentially the only major social activity in our small town. It was a place for kids to gather and learn to play baseball, and a time for our parents to come together to socialize and watch our games. I would say almost 90 percent of my good memories before I was rescued at the age of fifteen happened on those baseball diamonds. The league had one real baseball field just adjacent to Wawaloam School. It was brand new when I started to play there, and as a child, there was no more perfect a place for me than at that park. It had an outfield fence, a turf infield, and a concession stand where we would buy a pack of baseball cards for twenty-five cents, pop the gum in our mouths, and shuffle through them to see if we got any good players. For me, Red Sox players were all I wanted. I would always try to trade for them if I could. We had real dugouts at the new park, with metal benches for us to sit on. I will admit that early on, I sat on them a lot. My position was right field, if I was lucky, but mostly I was a benchwarmer. There were even small bleacher sections on each side of the field: one for the home team parents, and one for the visiting team parents. The senior league, a higher age group of mostly high school kids, played at Metcalf Field just up the road. This was just a huge sports field, with a baseball diamond in the far back right and a smaller Little League-sized diamond on the near right as you walked in from the parking lot. There were no fences, except for the backstops. If you hit one over an outfielder's head, it would roll for ages. At the end of the day, Little League was just good clean fun.

We were playing a game we loved with family and friends. I remember fondly all the days I spent practicing on those fields, the games, and the competition. I remember my father getting home from work and having my brother and I come out and play catch and do whiffle-ball batting drills for a couple hours each night. I do still love baseball and I am still a Red Sox fan, even if I do live thousands of miles away now.

And then there were the Cub Scouts. I think every small town has a scout troop of some kind. I remember sitting at Mrs. Salvail's house as a part of her Cub Scout den. I remember playing with Hot Wheels cars, STP racers, Evil Knievel toys, and watching the Mickey Mouse Club on a black-and-white television set in her living room. I don't remember much of the time I spent there anymore—just the toys I mentioned above. But I do remember it was fun. I also remember being part of a Webelo troop and how we met in the basement of the town hall to have pinewood racecar competitions and other activities. I remember running around that basement, spinning in circles around the support columns that ran from floor to ceiling, parents hollering for us to stop. They knew that we would just start all over again when they turned away, but appearances had to be kept. It was a good time, a good place to be, and it had a feeling of community. You felt you were important and belonged to something bigger than yourself. I know that there were 4H clubs and other activities in town, but I did not partake of any of those. I did, however, see the results of their labors at the county fair every year, later in life, when I was able to go. They looked like they loved what they were doing, and many of them still do it to this day.

West Greenwich was a quiet, residential town when I was a child, the kind of town where you commute out of town for work. There was no industry or businesses in town to speak of. What we did have were farms—strawberry fields, hayfields, and pumpkin patches. For many of the town's older children, Searle's Strawberry Farm would be the site of their first job. Classes would end for the day at Metcalf Middle School, and we would run across the street to pick strawberries for twenty-five cents a quart. We would kneel on the ground, peering into the rows of plants, hand-picking the ripe red strawberries. We would fill our buckets one at a time, and high school kids would keep track of how many quarts each of us had picked. The truth of the matter is that half of the ripe fruit would go into our mouths, not into the quart baskets. I honestly think we all ate more than we ever collected. Every day, at the end of picking time, we would all line up to get paid for what we had picked. Most of us had strawberry juice staining our faces, but none of us felt any shame about it. All we knew was that we were all a few quarters richer, and content in the innocence of youth.

Many years later, I learned the truth of this. All the clever, secret ways we had of popping a nice, plump, red strawberry into our mouths were a wasted effort. Mr. and Mrs. Searle knew what we were doing, and it gave them joy to see us happy. On a good day, I would get on the bus to go to school, finish school, run across the street to pick strawberries, then run back across for baseball practice. It was a good town, with good people, and the potential for oh-so-many good memories to be mixed in with the bad.

As I start to think on those good memories, it doesn't take long for an image of that old house to pop up in my mind and ruin things. Pain. Anger. Fear. So many savage memories of my childhood began there.

When I see a picture of that house now, I feel all that dread once again. I have an irrational fear that I might have to go back to that life again one day. I would rather die than live even one day of my old life again. Was my escape just a twisted dream? Will I wake up in that house, in that cellar, in that attic, in the dark, a scared child once again?

You see, in that house there are many ghosts. Ghosts of murdered, innocent, children's childhoods. Ghosts of the death of joy and loss of hope. Ghosts of dead self-worth and trust. The haunting howling of these ghosts that do not comprehend what happened to them still remain. They have been frozen in time, trapped. This house is a purgatory for all that was lost, and so many fragments remain there, trapped forever.

Long ago, I left that dark chapter of my life behind. When I see that house now, it astonishes me that there is no warning sign. There is no bright orange sign that, in clear, black, capital letters, reads: DANGER. I am amazed that it has not been marked on the map of West Greenwich with a huge X, with a picture of a stylized demon beside it, saying, *Warning: Here There Be Monsters.*

— 4 —

CHILDHOOD LOST

My childhood was taken from me. I want it back. Actually, to get it back implies I ever had one to begin with. I was robbed, deprived of a happy youth. I never received the opportunity to just be a normal kid in that house. I had to grow up so fast. I put aside childish things, I learned to survive hell while other kids learned to play tag. I learned to hide the pain and sorrow and bury my anger deep inside. I learned to never speak a word, to not even hint at what life was like for me and my sister Lisa. I told no one of the death of my childhood. To speak of it was unthinkable. In any case, who would have believed me if I had?

My childhood was a desert devoid of happiness. In fact, it would have been a total loss if not for the oasis of baseball. My father loved baseball, so I got to play—it is that simple. This is the only time I can remember where Lucille let my father make a decision she did not approve of. Lucille eventually gave in and allowed me to play, for appearance's sake. How strange it would look, if my stepbrother Michael played, but I did not. I played baseball to lend an appearance of normalcy in the public eye. So, on the surface, it looked like we were a normal family, a happy family.

If not for baseball, the only good memories I would have would be of Rocky Point Amusement Park. One day out of every year, we got to go there. Once a year, Ciba Geigy, the chemical company my father worked for, would rent out the entire park for a day. There would be games, rides, food, and friends. We would pack up as a family and go. Lucille had to take us along for appearance's sake, or the house of cards she had built out of lies and deception would fall down. The baseball months were the best few months of the year for me. I got to wear a clean uniform. I got to bathe. For just a little while, I got to look like a normal kid. I had to look normal, only because other parents were watching. Appearances had to be kept. Those are the good memories of my childhood, such as it was: baseball and Rocky Point.

The moment I got home from these "normal" activities it was back into the filthy, unwashed clothes and back to the forced labor that was my life. I want to be able to open a photo album full of pictures of the happy times, the good times, of smiles frozen in time by the miracle of Kodak. I want to be able to run old 9mm films of the good times and laugh at my hijinks from when I was a happy child.

But I have no past, no recorded history of my childhood. For me, my recorded history starts at fifteen, when I finally escaped from that house. For my sister Lisa, her life started at sixteen, when she escaped, as well. Lucille "lovingly" went through all the photo albums after we left with, a surgeon's eyes, removing all traces of our existence. She erased us. Lucille was finally able to expunge us from her life. Snapshots of my past might awaken memories of better times, but they are gone now, never to be seen again. Nothing remains of my childhood except memories. Memories of duct tape, a dark cellar, an attic, beatings, hunger, more hunger, even more hunger, so much pain—and, of course, being afraid of the dark.

— 5 —

THE PLAYERS

The great playwright Shakespeare once wrote, "All the world's a stage, and all the men and women merely players." With that great quote in mind, let me introduce the cast of players in the first act of my life. This is my soliloquy of remembrance.

How does one even begin to describe the enigma that was my stepmother, Lucille? Looking back now, with older eyes and with a lifetime of experience behind me, I can do nothing but feel pity for her. I also have a deep-seated emotional fear and loathing of her that borders on the neurotic. But she wasn't always that way. It started out so innocently. I think she really did try, at first. I don't think she intended to become the monster that she turned into. She seemed so normal and so pretty, on the surface, and appeared to be the perfect wife and mother to the outside world.

Lucille met my father, Dale, at a Parents Without Partners dance. Dale was a recent widower with three children—Lori, Lisa, and me. Lucille had recently been divorced and had twin children of her own, Monique and Michael. They hit it off and married soon after they met.

She was a real looker and had even done a couple modeling gigs when she was younger. My father honestly must have thought he had hit the lottery. Lucille got a husband and a father for her twins, and the plan was to raise them along with my sisters and me.

What I can remember from those very early years was that she could be loving, but at times it seemed she did not like me very much and was not happy I was underfoot. I recall she did make some effort in those early days; I really think she did. I remember a couple birthday parties at the picnic table that was on our backyard patio. The parties were for both Lisa and me, since our birthdays happened to be just a week apart. I remember games of Pin the Tail on the Donkey and a piñata being smashed to pieces. I remember a birthday cake and candles, and I recall smiles on the faces of one and all. I also remember other peculiar details, too, that at the time I didn't completely understand. For example, I was not allowed to invite friends to my party, like Monique and Michael did for theirs. These were small things, wrong things that you cannot fully comprehend as a child, but I could still sense there was an injustice in it, anyway.

Lucille was, above all other things, an excellent dresser. She always sported the newest fashions and always had perfect hair and makeup...always. That is what I remember about her most, how important appearances were to her. Just to set foot outside of the house required she invest two to three hours in the bathroom putting on her makeup and doing her hair. This ritual was performed for anything she did: sunbathing, driving to errands, shopping... literally, anything.

When she did go out, she was always happy and talkative with everyone she met. People seemed to genuinely like her. After all, she was a well-dressed, attractive woman. She loved to talk about antiques and she loved to talk about our "new" old house. Anyone who met her was impressed with how well-spoken and put together she was.

To the outside world, she appeared deeply devoted to her husband, Dale, and her children, Monique, and Michael. She would go to all

Monique's ballet lessons and performances, and she would come to every one of Michael's baseball games. Whenever Lucille came to the ballfield, she was always dressed to the nines, intending to flaunt it and outshine all the other mothers in the grandstand. She was always prepared to chat about Michael or Monique to the other parents or spectators, adeptly dodging any question about me or Lisa.

She loved to host family reunions and would invite everyone to Kitt's Tavern, put on a big feed, and then mix and mingle with our extended family, just soaking in the adoration that so many of her relatives felt for her.

Lucille was a stay-at-home mother and she never had to worry about a job or money, as everything was provided for by my father. Her parents, my Meme and Pepe, could walk on water in my eyes, and how Lucille could have been a product of such a sweet couple I have no idea. Through the years, I have had people mention to me that despite appearances, something always felt a bit off when they spoke with her. They said it felt as if danger signals were somehow emanating from her.

As early as I can recall, I remember the inequalities in our home. I knew who Mommy's favorites were, and Lisa, Lori, and I did not make that list. I could sense she was cold, uncaring, and even acted offended by me almost all the time. She loved a clean house; however, she did not like to clean. So as a result, she became the great delegator of chores. It started with Lori, when we lived at Myra Road; the sweeping, vacuuming, dishwashing, and most of the rest of the household chores became her responsibility alone. Lucille and Lori got along with each other like oil and water. Lisa and I were too young to do chores yet, but the division of love in the house that came from Lucille was distinct and recognizable to us even at a very young age.

As I write this, I realize I cannot adequately describe this woman who had such a huge and devastating effect on my life. How can that be? After all, she was my mother for thirteen years yet I never learned who she was. I do know that I do not have one happy memory, not a single fond memory, from any time that I spent alone with Lucille.

Me as a baby with cousin Tim and Lisa

How could I have lived thirteen years with my stepmother and not have a single happy memory of her in all that time?

My birth father, Dale, was an amazing person and a good dad in many of the ways that matter. He was born in Pennsylvania, where he played sports and would go home to a drunk dad who used to beat him for fun. He joined the US Navy, and when his enlistment finished, he settled in Rhode Island. He married and had four children with his first wife—my biological mother, Barbara. Barbara died of a cerebral thrombosis at the age of twenty-nine, leaving him alone with four children, including a newborn (me).

He worked at a chemical company to support his family. He mowed the lawn on weekends in the summer, shoveled snow in the winter, and had a honey-do list for the first two weeks of August every year when he was on holiday. In short, he provided and cared for his family, and I believe he even loved us—in his own way. Lucille's children included. But my father could never refuse Lucille, and despite his love for his own children, he would always comply with any of her sadistic requests above all else. So, like *Alice in Wonderland*, down the twisted rabbit hole of abuse we went. My sisters and I became sacrifices on the altar of whatever twisted love my father felt for his second wife.

Eventually, we moved away from Myra Road in Coventry to Weaver Hill Road in West Greenwich. By this time, our father had turned on my older sister, Lori, due to the constant nagging from Lucille about how bad a child she was. Simply put, he took sides and chose Lucille over Lori. This set a pattern that continued for years, long after Lori had finally given up and ran away.

Once we got to Weaver Hill, my father started to slowly change. He was always busy, working on the house or the property. In my mind, there was nothing my father could not do. Plaster a new ceiling? Dad can do it. Shingle the entire house, including the roof? Dad can do it. Put in a new flight of stairs? Yep, Dad can do that, too. I was, and I am, still envious of how no project or home repair crisis phased him—he just set his jaw and did what needed to be done. In my life, I have known few people who were truly a jack of all trades, master of all, but in my eyes, my father, Dale, was one.

As I got older, my father became Lucille's long arm of the law, her dispenser of justice, and her inflictor of pain. He still worked at the chemical company, but spent most of his off-time fixing up the house or coaching baseball. He was six-foot-two, kept himself in good shape, and was always up for a game of catch if the weather permitted. He was obsessed with me playing higher levels of baseball, so we would do whiffle ball batting practice, bunting drills, and shag fly balls for hours on end. I know he loved me, but in the end, he simply valued Lucille more.

I know my father was acutely afraid of losing another wife. Lucille was painfully aware of this fact, too, and used it to her benefit. She manipulated him into beating his own children, using his deep-seated fear of losing her as a weapon. The saying "this will hurt me more than you" became his mantra when he beat me, again and again.

My stepbrother Michael was a sickly child when he was young. He suffered from asthma, and it was quite severe. I remember the ambulance sirens screaming as the emergency rig pulled up to the curb of our house on Myra Road. I have flashes of memory of that incident that took place in our living room. Michael collapsed on the floor; he could not breathe. I was able to peer over the couch and I remember thinking he was dying. I was told to leave the room as they got him ready for transport to the hospital, and the memory ends there. After that, we would make trips to St. Joseph's Hospital so Michael could get shots to help with his asthma attacks.

In those early days, we got along together like you'd expect most little boys would: we played with G.I. Joes, toy soldiers, Hot Wheels, cap guns, and squirt guns. We rode our Big Wheels, read Mother Goose books, and wrecked our sisters' Barbies. We would watch Saturday morning cartoons every week, all three hours of them. We would lay on the carpet in the living room soaking in every show with childlike rapture. I know the younger generation does not realize how much the world has changed, but Saturday morning was *it*, there were no more cartoons for the rest of the week. But in its place, we had comic books and the Sunday morning newspaper comics pages. The rest of the time, we would be outside in the yard, playing with the neighborhood kids.

We bickered as brothers often do, but when the fight eventually evolved enough to the "I'm telling Mom!" stage, as it occasionally would, we would march into the house and plead our cases to Lucille. These disputes were about whose turn it was to use a toy, or some other trivial disagreement. And invariably, Lucille would always side with Michael. I didn't understand why I was always in the wrong. And this was the first recollection I had of going to my room for the night without dinner.

Even at a very young age, Michael was very charismatic. He was a ringleader of the neighborhood kids. He organized and ran the games, like hide-and-seek or tag, or he would get us to all run around pretending to be cops and robbers or cowboys and Indians. He had another favorite game that we called "Pig Pile on David and Tickle Him Until He Pees." Lucky me. It was all based on the demographics of our neighborhood, I assumed. I was the youngest, therefore it was my job to be at the bottom of the pile. This important neighborhood duty also involved being forced to eat worms, mud pies, and a plethora of other delightful earthly creations.

When we first started to go to school in Coventry, Michael became even more popular. He always seemed to be surrounded by a crowd of admirers. He was even the king of the boys at kindergarten recess (because girls were gross, of course). When we moved to West Greenwich, Michael thrived there, as well. The recess pecking order changed a bit, but not by much. Michael was always ready to kick someone off the swing set so he could use it, and few complained. In short, Michael was popular, well-dressed, clean, and charismatic. When he moved up to middle school, his status as Mr. Popularity only improved.

The American Bicentennial happened when we were in the fourth grade (cue the fireworks). That was the first year Michael and I were eligible to play in the Exeter–West Greenwich Little League. Michael's hand-eye coordination advanced faster than mine, and he advanced from the farm league to the majors the next year. He shined as a baseball player, while I shined the bench with my backside. (But I was damned good at it.) Due to league rules, I got pushed up to the same majors' team as Michael. The rule had something to do with parents having two kids on two different teams, which would be too much of a burden. Michael's life revolved around school, baseball, hanging out with friends, and hitting on girls.

Michael had it all in my eyes: good mates, good clothes, and hell, he even had a bedroom in the main part of the house. He also knew he lived an entitled life compared to me, because we used to talk about it. He would say he didn't understand why we were treated so differently, but he told me he was afraid that if he said anything to Lucille about it, she would start in on him. Shortly after he started high school, Lucille brought him to a hair stylist to get his hair permed, and I must admit, he looked sharp. I will even admit I was jealous of his Izod sweaters and Farah pants. Michael was only given the best clothing to wear. When he started dating, all the pretty girls wanted to go out with him.

I have learned something about families as I have grown older: siblings normally stand up for each other. Hell, they even defend each other. Yes, they might fight like cats and dogs, but heaven help any outsider if they decide to pick on one of us. "Don't mess with kin." "Blood is thicker than water." "We defend our own." Sadly, this was not the dynamic between Michael and me. Not once did he ever stand up to the bullies who tortured me, or even attempt to help me. The bullies all liked Michael—respected him, even. He could have easily stopped the abuse with a few well-placed words. But he knew could not deign to tarnish his reputation by speaking up for a woeful creature like me. In his mind, I was not a real brother to him. In fact, most of the school staff and students did not even realize we were brothers.

What I can recall most about my stepsister Monique are Barbie dolls, the ballet, Danskin leotards, dance slippers, and toe shoes. As far back as I can remember she was always going to ballet classes and performing in dance recitals. I think that, like most little boys who have little sisters, I did not spend much time playing with her when we were very young. I did not want to play with Barbie dolls like Monique did. We had no common interests when it came to playtime. I played with Tonka trucks in the sandbox our father had made for us, and she played with her Barbies. I moved onto G.I. Joe and still, she played with Barbies. On rainy days, we might spend some time in the basement of Myra Road playing checkers and other assorted and long-forgotten board games. Boys being boys, and girls being girls, we just did not have much in common.

When we first moved, our dynamic stayed the same for a while. Then she went to school and started to become one of the popular, pretty girls. We were in different classes and had different teachers. At recess time, I watched her play with the other girls, doing cartwheels, somersaults, and laughing like only a child at play can laugh.

When we went to middle school, Monique started to come into her own. She was pretty, she was a dancer, she wore nice clothes, she had the nicest hair, and she was popular. She would don her leotards and perform on the stage for school events, always gravitating toward the center of attention. She could draw some of the best pictures in art class, too. This annoyed me, as I could not even write legibly, never mind draw a pretty picture. In my eyes, Monique had it all.

Then, along came our high school days. I went to public school and Monique went to St. Xavier Academy, a private, all-girls school. Because of the different schools, we did not see much of each other at all in those years. The ballet also became very much the driving force in her life. She studied at Myles Marsden's School of Ballet and she loved it...so many practices, so many recitals. I learned to love watching the ballet during this time. I still do.

Now comes a bit of a sticky wicket for me, as I think about my stepsister Monique; I honestly don't know what to think of her anymore. I have never had any anger toward her, and I still don't think I do. Is it resentment that I feel toward her, now? She never intentionally hurt me or instigated anyone to harm me, but as I think about this more and more, she is not without guilt. She saw what was going on, she knew the wrongness of it all, and she did nothing. We spoke of it from time to time, and I know she was afraid to speak up. I suppose Lucille, being what she was, could have turned on her in a heartbeat, too.

But as I look at this now, I can see it for the excuse it was. Lucille would never, *ever* turn on her own precious twins—no chance in hell. Monique sat in her patio sunbathing chair getting the perfect tan, hanging out in the pool, swimming with her friends, and listening to music on the radio. She had it all. (If you think I sound jealous, it is because I am.) Angora sweaters, salon hairstyles, and private school are just a few things I remember.

When our father Dale died, Monique told me in a private message that Dale Harter was the best man she ever knew and that he had to make some hard choices in his life. I call shenanigans—abusing and forcing all three of your biological children out of your life to please your new wife is not a hard choice.

I never got to know my brother, Dale Jr. I would have loved to have seen the man he would have become. I could have used a big brother to look up to who would look after me—and whom I could annoy, as little brothers are prone to do. But it was not meant to be. I was only eleven days old on the day of his tragic death, and he was only seven years old at the time. I know so very little of my brother, as my father never spoke of him—not once. So, I need to use my imagination to create the day he met me for the first time. Did he look down into my crib and touch my face, greeting his new baby brother? I would like to think he did. A few fleeting moments of brotherly contact before he was gone forever.

Dale Jr. was born with severely clubbed feet. Clubfoot is a common birth defect that affects both the muscles and bones. Instead of being straight, a clubfoot points down and turns in. This twisting causes the toes to point toward the opposite leg. A baby can be born with the defect in one or both feet, and in Dale Jr.'s case, it affected both his feet. As a result, Dale Jr. wore metal and leather braces with special shoes that were prescribed to correct this condition. The doctors adjusted the braces in small increments over time, and eventually, his condition improved. After a while, he no longer needed the braces. He was finally able to run and jump like a normal child. I cannot imagine the joy he must have felt. Sadly, this joy was short lived; he enjoyed less than a week without the braces before his death.

Dale Jr. died on a bright, sunny day on September 9th, 1966. He went out for a bike ride along Myra Road, did a jump off the sidewalk into the street, and was struck by a car and killed. He was thrown from his bike onto a neighbor's yard. He died in this poor stranger's arms as she held him, waiting for the ambulance to arrive. The driver happened to be a US Marine home on leave from Vietnam. No charges were ever filed, as the death was determined to be accidental. It was just a random, tragic accident that prevented my brother and me from getting to know one another. I have two tiny black-and-white snapshots of Dale Jr. These photos are all I have of him.

In one of the sheds at Kitt's Tavern, there was an old, red, Schwinn bike that was a little bent up but kept in a safe place all the same. I learned later that it was my brother's bike—my father never threw it away. I don't think he could bear to get rid of the last thing he had left in the world of his son. One day, I also found Dale Jr's braces in a box in the shed. I did not know what they were or who they belonged to. I did not know until years later, when a relative told me that Dale Jr. had worn them.

I know even less about my mother, Barbara Harter, than I do of my brother, Dale Jr. All I have left of her is my life, my name, and a single picture on a bookshelf. She was so beautiful. She had long blonde hair and blue eyes. I would love to have gotten to know her, but fate decided that this was not meant to be. My mother, Barbara, died the same day I was born. She died of complications from a car accident that happened right before my birth. This accident took place at the busy intersection of Arnold Road and Tiogue Avenue in Coventry, not too far from the house. At the time of the accident, there was only a stop sign there—no traffic lights had been installed.

Dale and Barbara had met at a dance at The Girls City Club and they started dating soon after. Her family had decided to move to upstate New York, and she did not want to go; she was so desperate to remain where she considered home. She had two suitors at the time, and my father gave her a ring first. She was able to stay in Rhode Island because she married my father. They had a no-frills wedding, tying the knot in the office of the clerk of the court. My mother, Barbara, worked at a bank and I was told she was well liked by her co-workers and customers. She gave birth to four children, including me, and from all accounts she was a sweet and loving mother. To her friends and family, her nickname was Sister, but to my siblings she was Mommy. I would have loved to have called her that.

She had been unhappy for the last few years of her marriage, with good reason. My mother had petitioned for divorce before becoming pregnant with me because my father cheated on her and had a child with another woman. According to my mother's brother, Uncle Bud, Dale also wanted her to become involved in a swinger's lifestyle

Harter family pic, left to right: Dale Jr, Barbara, Lisa, Dale Sr, Lori. My mother is pregnant with me in this picture.

with him. My mother wanted nothing to do with the wife-swapping lifestyle and distrusted my father deeply for it. But when she became pregnant with me, she withdrew the petition, happy she was having another child and willing to give my father one more chance.

I did not know Dale had allowed Lucille to adopt us for a very long time. I had always thought Lucille was my mother. Yes, I knew Michael and Monique had a different last name, but it had always been that way and I was too little to understand what that meant. Then one day, I was digging through an old box in Lucille's shed and I found something very strange. It was a Rhode Island driver's license from a woman whose name was Barbara Harter. I was very confused about this, so I asked my sister, Lisa, who the woman was. Lisa looked at me bewildered and said, "David, that's our mother!" I did not understand what she meant at first, then it hit me like a sucker punch—I was floored.

Later in the day, I asked my father if Barbara Harter was, in fact, my real mother. He looked at me with contempt and he said, with venom in his voice, that yes, she was my mother, and that I had killed her. He looked me over with so much anger in his eyes, then turned and walked away. This information cut me to pieces. I cried myself to sleep for weeks after that. I knew that the subject was taboo, and I never asked again. I carried so much guilt about it from that day forward… so much guilt.

I never got to meet my mother, and this has left a hole in my heart my entire life. Is it possible to miss someone that you never knew? Yes, it is.

My sister, Lori, was larger than life to me when I was a little boy. I idolized her. She had her own room in the finished basement at Myra Road when no one else did. She was my big sister, and though just a kid herself, she seemed so grown up to me. I have so many random memories of her from back then. Lori had a small fish tank that was home to a goldfish named "S." There was a sculpture on her dresser made of beach rocks glued together to look like a rock band. She had felt posters on the wall of her room that would glow when she turned on her black lights. She had her very own record player and a collection of 45 rpm records, a whole carrying case full of them. I used to love to sit in her room and listen to her play her music. She loved The Beatles and played them all the time. I learned to love those songs back then, too. She had one 45 by Three Dog Night, *Joy to the World*. She would play it over and over for me while I tried to sing along in my childlike falsetto, singing, "Jerimiah was a bullfrog, was a good friend of mine, never understood a single word he said, but I helped him a-drink his wine." Any time I hear this song, even to this very day, it carries me back to that bedroom where I listened to the record player with my big sister.

Lori ran away when she was seventeen. I didn't get to see her again for several years. I missed her, but children are adaptive, and I moved on. Lori got married and rented an apartment in Pawtucket, Rhode Island. I remember Lucille sitting us down to tell us that Lori had invited us all over for Christmas, but she thought we should stay home with "our" family and not get involved with Lori again. This was discussed at a huge family meeting in the kitchen, where everyone had an

Lori dancing with my father at her wedding

opportunity to speak their mind. I said I wanted to see Lori, thinking to myself that she was my sister, so what was the problem? I did get to go over and spend the night with Lori and her husband, Gary, a few times. God, I loved that place—shag carpets, lava lamps, velvet posters of dragons with black lights, and even a Kiss pinball machine in the kitchen. Sound tacky? It was, but I still loved that apartment. In Lori's defense, it was the seventies, folks, and the psychedelic look was in style. Disco shirts, bell-bottoms, and Converse All-Stars just came with the times.

Time passed, and Lori and I grew apart. In later years, Lori went even further down the rabbit hole of addiction. I do not know the full extent of what Lori went through as a child with Lucille and Dale as her parents, but I can guess it was not too dissimilar to what Lisa and I experienced.

Lori's escape was heroin. She got hooked and was never able break free. She started to do things to support her heroin addiction like sex work and selling drugs. There was nothing she wouldn't do to acquire more heroin. Lori was caught in a trap, as most addicts are. Lori spent several years in jail, remaining addicted the entire time. When she got out on parole, she moved back to her apartment in Pawtucket and started the cycle all over again.

Many years later, I managed to find out where she lived and drove over to visit her there. I walked into the apartment and was just stunned. There was a huge bag of over one thousand valium pills just sitting on the table in plain sight. The apartment was filthy and it stunk. I could hear my newborn nephew David crying in the other room. Lori was so jittery—happy to see me, but ever so jittery. One of her friends dropped by and Lori told me she needed to go into the bathroom for a minute to get her fix. I asked her to wait until I left, but she could not. In the bathroom she went with her friend, a bag of heroin, and one needle. I was so very angry with her. I was watching her kill herself right in front of me. She came out of the bathroom all happy and chatty, but I had to leave; I could not be there anymore. Over the next couple years, from time to time, I would hear she was working the streets again, and off I would go, patrolling the streets of Pawtucket, looking for my sister so I could convince her to go to rehab one more time.

After a few years of this, Lori got busted and her parole was revoked. A deal was struck for her to go into a one-year rehab program with Marathon House Treatment Center. She did so well for eleven months. I got to visit her and see her sober once every two weeks for almost a year. I got to meet her daughters, Jennifer and Tiffany when they visited as well, who were such sweet little girls. I was convinced Lori had beaten her addiction at last; she had a job as a travel agent and was doing so well. Everything was good. Then, suddenly, it all went bad. Lori went out for a smoke, her boyfriend pulled up in his car, she jumped in, and they drove away.

I did not hear from her for several years. I had to assume she was dead or in jail again. At this point, I made one of the hardest decisions of my life. I had to let her go and be who she wanted to be, not what

I wanted of her. I visited her once with my sister Lisa not long before she passed away. Years of heroin abuse and methadone maintenance had disabled her. She seemed like an empty shell of a person. Nothing that remained there was my sister. The bright-eyed girl I used to sing with in the basement at Myra Road was gone. She eventually died of an overdose, alone in bed at sixty-one years of age. My sister's pain and emotional suffering came to a sad end. I grieve for the happy girl that lives in my memory, playing The Beatles and just being my big sister.

I have one blood sibling left now: my sister Lisa. Woe to any person who ever hurts her, as I promise there will be a price to pay and I will hand them the bill in blood. My memories of Lisa when I was a child are incomplete. What I do remember from the early days are pigtails, Barbie dolls, and Golden Books with a 45 rpm record in them. I remember the gingerbread man, The Game of Life, and reading Mother Goose books together. I remember sitting on the couch with her in the basement watching television, then sitting on the same couch later with Lisa and our dad as he read us a Dr. Suess book. I remember *One Fish, Two Fish, Red Fish, Blue Fish, Green Eggs and Ham,* and so many other books from our early childhood that we shared. And I remember being chased out of the "girls' room," as boys were not welcome or allowed. But that's just brothers and sisters being what they are: confrontational at all costs, pushing the limit every day, and testing each other. Sorry to say, but many Barbie dolls and G.I. Joes were harmed in the making of our childhood.

I remember once walking to school as a group when we were little. Lisa was balancing herself on the decorative brick edge of the lawn as we walked, and then she fell, hitting her head on the sharp edge of the bricks. She was bleeding all over the place. We all ran home to tell our mother. Lucille's response was to get mad and shout at her. Lisa ended up with several stitches, if I recall. That memory has faded so much over time.

On more routine days, Lisa and I would walk home after school with the other kids and would run up to talk to our mailman. He loved to talk to all of us, and he would walk along the sidewalk with a gaggle of us kids following him. He knew us all by name. Times were so different then.

Lisa was initially such a happy kid. She had a home where she belonged and a Daddy who loved her. I do not remember any especially bad times for her at Myra Road. Did Monique and Michael have nicer things? Well, yes, they did, but at that age, we didn't have red flags going up about why they had all the better toys. After all, who cared? Lisa and I had the whole outside world as a playground, and the imagination and wonder of a child to keep us happy.

— 6 —

PAINT CHIPS

I was so damned young. I was so damned naïve. My oldest sister, Lori, was now gone from the house. She had finally had enough of being treated like she was less than human. She ran away from her own hell on earth. When Lori fled, Lucille lost her favorite victim. Her eyes then turned to Lisa and me. Lucille started to treat us like she had treated Lori. To her, we were subhuman drones, tailor-made receptacles for her abuse. We were not her blood-related children, and just the sight of us seemed to offend her. We were just unwanted toys for her to play with and destroy. In my mind, I thought we had done something wrong. I had no idea why she was so mad at us. But it had to be my fault, right? Parents are supposed to have a good reason to do what they do with their children. So, I came to the youthful conclusion that I was not a good boy. I knew that if I could prove to her that I was a good boy, she might love me some day. So, I set out trying to do things, small things, that I thought might eventually make her smile, but nothing seemed to work.

I was afraid of Lucille from the start, but I still loved her, as she was the only mother I had ever known. Little boys are supposed to love their mothers, are they not? I was desperate to find something, anything to make her happy with me somehow. So many years of pain later, I realized one pertinent, all-encompassing fact: Lori, Lisa, and I were not, and would never be, treated like her own children. No amount of effort would ever have changed that fact. I did not yet fully understand that we were not blood of her blood, bone of her bone.

Lucille's true love and pride and joy was Kitt's Tavern, but there was one flaw in it that she did not know how to solve. She hated the many layers of paint on the original woodwork in the house. She could not figure out how to safely remove the paint down to the original wood without damaging it. This vexed her. She tried several times to find a solution to this problem. Lightly tapping with a screwdriver, eventually she chipped a small hole into the paint. After all those years, the original wood stain was still under there. Underneath all of those copious layers of paint was the stain that was used when the house was first built. Lucille was both excited and dismayed; she had found something she thought was amazing, but had found no way to do anything about it. It would take years to remove all of that paint one chip at a time. So, Lucille and our father finally decided they were going to have to paint over everything again. The colors would be period-correct, but in paint, not in the stain that would have been on the original woodwork. As I furtively watched Lucille chip that small hole into the paint, I had a eureka moment. I waited until she left the room, then I went up to the door and ran my fingernail over the edge of the paint. Tiny chips came off on my nail, and I came up with an idea.

I was excited by my idea. It seemed so simple, yet it might work… might. Not being sure of success was a problem for me. I knew that if I made it worse, there would be hell to pay with Lucille. So, I waited for a day where she went out to run errands to try my plan. With a great amount of trepidation, I grasped one of my father's putty knives and started to carefully scrape off some of the paint on the pantry door, where Lucille had made the first small, chipped hole. I experimented on how to use the putty knife and found that if I held it at a certain angle while I pulled down, pressing hard, the paint would chip right off without damaging the wood underneath. It appeared to me that removing the centuries of paint layers was feasible but would take copious amounts of time to carefully chip it all away. The wood that was being revealed was beautiful, glowing, with a bright red wood stain. I loved what it looked like; I was quite proud of myself, actually. I had found a solution to Lucille's problem. She would be so proud of me, and love me again for sure this time.

By the time Lucille returned home, I had meticulously scraped an area of about six inches by twelve inches off the door. She pulled into the driveway, and I was suddenly terrified as the realization struck me that she would now see what I had done. I now believed she was going to get mad and start to scream at me. I sat there among the chips on the floor and thought the worst. It was what I had come to expect from Lucille: always the worst possible reaction, with just a dash of kindness tossed in occasionally, just to make the punishments seem even crueler and more confusing. I lived in mortal fear of disappointing her. Lucille had to be pleased at all costs, and at all times. When she walked into the house, I was sitting nervously at the dining room table. I was doing my best invisible man impression, which I had learned as a younger child. I was so scared I was afraid to breathe. Always the little informer, my stepbrother Michael took it upon himself to show Lucille what I had done, hoping he would get me in trouble.

She looked at the spot I had cleared of paint very carefully. She then looked at me and smiled, asking if I had done this and how I had done it. She looked so pleased with me, that I popped up out of my chair to show her my technique. I took the putty knife and cleared more of the paint, and explained to her that it was easy, it just took a lot of time. All I needed was that putty knife to scrape off all that old paint.

We all make innocent seeming choices in our lives, choices with unforeseen consequences that we wish we could undo. The choice I made on that rainy day I would come to regret. I wish I had never scraped the paint off that pantry door. That one choice of mine was pure of heart, to try to please an unloving stepmother. I wanted to make her love me. But the choice to scrape the paint that day had consequences I could never have foreseen. Lisa and I ended up paying for that choice in blood, sweat, and tears for years to come. In my mind, this was the day that everything changed for the worse in that house. Our childhood ended for good that day.

There was no coming back. When Lucille saw what I had done, she knew she had finally found a use for us. It cemented her view that Lisa and I could become a free and accessible labor force: personal slaves to do her bidding, to make her dream house vision become a reality. We had no choice but to do everything we were told to do. She knew our weaknesses. The price of refusal was too high.

From then on, in the cold weather from morning until nightfall, I stood there with a putty knife between my little fingers and scraped the paint off of every door and frame in that huge building, then scraped it off all of the woodwork around the rest of the house. I never stopped, no matter how sore my arm or hands got. Lucille might be, and probably was, lurking around a corner, waiting to scream in my ear, trying to rip my ear off my head as she liked to do. If I did not work up to her standards, supper would be denied me or I would be banished to the attic. Then our father would get home from work and Lucille would get her payment in full for my laziness, as my father would beat me at her request. I would then have to climb into my filthy bed, with no supper, covered in sweat from work and sore from my punishment. Then there was the next day. The next day. The next day. And the day after that. There was no end in sight.

As I scraped, Lisa would be working on her insane list of household chores. As she did them, Lucille would regularly sneak up behind Lisa to check on her work, wooden spoon in hand as she stalked. If Lisa, according to Lucille, had nothing to do, she was reassigned to come and help me scrape, scrape, and scrape. There were more than two hundred years of paint layers being removed in chips, and all sorts of paint dust floating around our faces. We had no face masks to prevent us from breathing it all in.

I felt so guilty. All this was happening because I thought I was helping. I was only trying to make my stepmother love me. And instead, all I did that day was show how we were inanimate tools she could use to achieve her ends. I regret the choice that I made so innocently that day; it led to so much pain.

I have been asked many times over the years how this all could have happened in plain sight of so many supposedly intelligent people, family members, and neighbors. The answer is really quite simple: no one wants to believe the truth. It is as simple as that. It was easier to believe that we did not like to bathe, that we were clumsy, that our bruises came from bumping into things and roughhousing, or that the bullies at school caused all the injuries on display. It was easier to believe we were awful children that had to be punished all of the time. *They must be such a trial for that nice lady Lucille and her wonderful husband.* Lucille was such a master manipulator who could spin a web of lies so convincing she would have people feeling sorry for her.

In the early stages of my abuse, people did notice things from time to time, but Lucille was prepared to answer any questions with logical and reasonable-sounding excuses. Mr. Sposato, my third-grade teacher, noticed the paint chips around my eyes and became concerned enough to call home about it. The dangers associated with lead paint were a big deal and in the news at the time, as it was learned that it caused severe developmental issues and learning difficulties in children. Lucille told him I had a bad habit of eating paint chips and that she could not break me of it. She told him she would be happy to keep a closer eye on me from now on. Lucille certainly did keep a closer eye on me after that. She made sure my face was clean of paint chips every morning before I got on the bus for school.

Our closest neighbor, Mr. Renihan, noticed the disparity of how the children were treated on our property, and was quite vocal about it to our father. The difference in clothing, cleanliness, and how Lisa and I worked while my stepbrother and stepsister played—he saw it all, and would quite literally yell at our father about it from across the property line. Mr. Renihan did not bend to Lucille's lies; he simply did not believe her. He once called the police thinking that they could do something to rectify our situation. But sadly, the police listened to Lucille and our father instead. The police would drive away, shaking their heads about crazy old Mr. Renihan. Not once did they actually speak to us, the children, the victims, and ask us what was going on.

But to be honest, even if they had asked, I am certain that Lisa and I both would have supported everything our parents had told the police. We were both mortally afraid of our parents. There had been too many beatings, too many twisted punishments, and an instilled belief that we were never going to get away from them. The police had to leave eventually, and we would pay for anything we told them with blood and pain. In my mind, the police could not help. No one could. I knew some people were trying to get something done about our situation, yet I sensed, deep down, that nothing would ever work or help. Lucille had an answer for everything, and a plan for every eventuality. We knew in our hearts that we could not beat her. That knowledge was hardwired into us as much as potty training had been instilled in us as toddlers.

— 7 —

FOOD AS A WEAPON

I am obsessed with food. I love food. I adore food. There are just not enough descriptive adjectives in the English language to express my love of food. However, because of childhood abuses and conditioning by Lucille, I have developed a lifelong problem with food. My problem is I do not have an off switch. When it comes to the consumption of food, there is never enough. Hand me a giant bag of chips and I will eat the whole bag. *Hope you did not want me to save any, so sorry.* There is no need to ask me if I am "going to eat that." I always do. I eat like the food in front of me is my last meal on earth. You see, for years, I honestly did not know when I was going to eat again. I was always so hungry. Now even the mere sight of food can bring back horrible memories of suffering, pain, and humiliation.

Food is supposed to bring families together. It is meant to be a celebration of life, and its bounty forms lasting memories for those involved in the meal.

I have memories of the great Thanksgiving dinner I had when I was ten, with all the fixin's. I recall watching Meme scurry around the kitchen, putting the final master strokes on a massive culinary feast. The mouthwatering smells wafting out of the oven were heavenly. I can still remember the smell of that freshly cooked turkey to this very day. Many years later, I easily recall the time I sat down at a club with my sister, Lisa, and her soon-to-be husband, David. Just having a beer, pizza, and a few wings while watching the Patriots game when I visited them is such a good memory. Food anchors so many of my memories, both good and bad. Quantity is a problem...what is too much? And I always want it, as it gives me comfort. In my youth, there was no guarantee when the next meal would come. Would I get enough to eat today? Would it be enough to curb the constant hunger that was growing inside of me?

Lucille used food as a weapon in her arsenal of abuse, simple as that. As far back as I can remember, meals were withheld as punishment for supposed crimes against Lucille. "Go to bed with no supper, David." "You are a bad boy, David." "You do not deserve to eat today, David." I never knew what I had done wrong; explanations were never forthcoming. I remember Lucille going obsessively through the pantry at Kitt's Tavern every day, taking inventory of the food we had on hand with a pad she kept well-hidden from curious eyes. She inventoried every cracker and cookie, every edible item in the house, so she could tell if I had "stolen" food from her. I remember her staring out the windows and skulking around the corners of the outbuildings. She was always trying to catch me, to see if I dared try so much as to steal a tomato out of the garden or try to take a drink of water out of the hose without consent. Yes, I needed her permission to even take a sip from the hose. No consent meant I was stealing her water.

Food was Lucille's weapon of choice, and she wielded it like a master. It was her double-edged sword—one edge was for me, and the other edge was for Lisa. For me, it was simple: Lucille would withhold food as punishment. "Oh, David, you did not finish your chore list in time? You must not have wanted supper, I guess. So sad." These lists would have a week's worth of chores listed around the property that had to be done in one day. If the list was not completed, I did not earn my supper. Instead, I got to go outside and work on some more chores, then go to bed hungry. My constant companions were the echoing growls of my empty stomach. I learned, over time, the items she tended to overlook while doing her food "inventory" and would sneak small amounts to try to get by—a teaspoon of sugar, a pinch of alfalfa sprouts, a spoonful of cottage cheese, and maybe a pinch of bran might be all I would be able to eat for the day. I did not do this too often, as she was always lurking and creeping around the corners, always jumping out at us when she thought she had caught us breaking one of her ridiculous rules.

Hunger was her method of control over me, and by God, it worked. I worked harder, and faster, but still never could get those lists done. I thought I might get the credit for trying hard and be rewarded with being allowed to eat dinner with the family. Sometimes, it worked. Most times, it did not.

For Lisa it was different, so very different. Lucille decided to fatten her up like a pig ready for the slaughterhouse. She fed her diet pills as stimulants and then valium, intentionally messing up her metabolism with horrible results. Then Lucille made Lisa eat vast quantities of food. It was an obvious planned attack to make her gain weight. All of this was done to make her look less desirable than our stepsister, Monique, and look less like our birth mother, Barbara. We did not understand all this at the time, but it is obvious to me now, in hindsight.

Lucille bought Little Debbie dessert snack cakes from the grocery store by the boxload, ten or twelve boxes at a time. These cakes were for Lisa's consumption only, and she was required to eat half a box at a time. She also made Lisa eat extra-large portions of food at every meal. Insane, overflowing plates were placed in front of her every night, and she had to eat every bit, down to the last crumb. Lucille then forced Lisa to eat more food and snack cakes every few hours in between meals, to keep her stomach full. "Here, take this valium. Now here, take this diet pill." I watched this happen almost every day. Heaven help Lisa if she could not or would not eat it all. Lucille would stand there with a huge wooden spoon and smack her on the back of the head and neck to make her eat more.

On the worst days, the inevitable would happen and Lisa would vomit. Lucille would then force her to eat her own vomit until she kept it all down.

I once remember Lisa and I sitting together, each with a container of rotten tomatoes. I had been told to pick the tomatoes the day before from the garden and was instructed not to miss a single ripe one. I picked them all, but then we had a hard frost that night that killed the leftover crop. This was a normal occurrence in the northeast, nothing to see here: "Farming in New England 101—The Beginner's Class." But Lucille noticed the rotting tomatoes in the patch and decided Lisa and I would have to eat them. She told us that we could not leave the table until every last rotten tomato was consumed. She was not going to stand by and let us waste food. In the end, I was able to finish mine, gagging all the while but managing to keep it all down. But Lisa could not and vomited hers up. To this day, a mere whiff of vomit brings flashbacks to that moment. I remember Lucille screaming at Lisa as she retched, then I remember Lucille beating her with a wooden spoon on her ears, neck, and head. Then she demanded that Lisa eat the vomit. Lisa tried, but kept throwing up again, begging to be allowed to stop. But Lucille kept saying that Lisa was wasting food and she would make her eat it until it was gone. There was no mercy to be found. This would be shocking to most people if it had happened just once, but it happened many times with different foods, spoiled or not.

One day I was given only one job. ("One job" according to Lucille, that is.) I was supposed to sweep the dining room floor and, as expected, I failed at it. If you have ever lived in an old colonial house, you know one thing about sweeping old wooden floors: no matter how much you sweep up, there always seems to be more dust and dirt in the cracks. It is almost mystical how it just never seems to end. Lucille pulled me by the ear into the room and sat me in a chair and made me watch her as she took the angle broom and dug in deep to get the dirt from the cracks to come out. She scooped up her prize in a dustpan and then asked me what I thought should happen to the dirt she had found. How could she make me remember not to do a bad job while sweeping next time? Just then, Lucille had a sadistic revelation and my punishment was decided. I would have to eat the dirt in the dustpan. I looked in the dustpan and saw a plastic bristle from the broom in the tray among the nastiness. I pulled it out of the tray, but Lucille told me—with that smirk I came to hate so much—that I had to eat that as well. This was the most vile and disgusting thing I have ever had to consume in my life. Then I got to eat dirt, more dirt, and was made to chew on it. The dirt grinding between my teeth was so uncomfortable and unpleasant. I was not allowed to drink any water to wash the dirt out of my mouth and forced myself to choke those sweepings down. After my tears began to fall, Lucille took pity on me and did not make me finish the entire dustpan full. I got to tip a bit into the rubbish bin instead of my mouth.

I know people will say, "Well I wouldn't have eaten that." I know for a fact they will say this, because I have heard it before. But they were not there. They did not live with the constant, overpowering fear of pain and punishment that we lived with. They did not live with the lack of choice. There was no choice for us but to comply. I was just a little kid. What was I supposed to do? I had been conditioned by nothing but pain and fear to that point of my life. To say "no" was never an option. To do what I was told was my only choice—if, in fact, having no choice is a choice at all.

Lisa used to hide some of her food from Lucille, making it appear as if she had eaten it. She had different locations in the house and kitchen to hide this food, including the space behind the double oven. Lisa would try to sneak some of the hidden food to me. I was glad to destroy the evidence for her, as I was always hungry. But unfortunately, eagle-eyed Lucille always managed to find the stashes or the wrappers, and Lisa would be severely beaten with that wooden spoon every time. I do not even think that wooden spoon was for cooking. It was so big; it was almost like a movie prop in the perfect kitchen display. How can one human being do such a thing to another human being, let alone their own child? I mean, it is not reasonable to beat a child with a paddle the size of a cricket bat if they are caught stealing a Ritz Cracker, right?

Now I am going to bring up an issue that I feel is important and integral to the very heart of what happened to us in that house: we did not deserve this. Nothing we did could ever justify what was done to us. Lisa and I were good kids. No, we were not perfect—no child is—but we were good children. How could we not be well behaved? The price was too high if we even thought of acting out. We were too afraid to do anything wrong. To even contemplate breaking a rule was unthinkable. We knew that the punishments that were passed out for even the smallest infraction never fit the crime. These punishments were sadistic, brutal, and psychologically damaging, and something we tried to avoid at all costs.

Now that I got the elephant in the room out of the way, I will say, yes, we did break rules at times. Lucille's sadistic rules were only for our father's children, not her precious twins. They were such destructive rules that we had to break them sometimes, just to survive in the insane world we lived in. Did I sneak food? Yes, I did. I was so hungry and I had so much work to do. Did Lisa hide food? She sure did—too much was too much, and she physically could eat no more. Did we break any other rules? Absolutely not. We were well-trained service animals. We submissively did our master's bidding to avoid the psychological lashes that refusal would always bring.

— 8 —

MEMORIES OF THE COLOR RED

Have you ever noticed that the strangest things can trigger an old memory? The smell of burning wax from a candle might remind you of a certain birthday party when you were a child, a happy moment with laughter, ice cream, and cake. The sound of a song playing on the radio brings back memories from middle school the first time you got up the guts to ask a girl to a dance and were shot down. Or the sound of a seagull's cry in the distance reminds you of the ocean, bringing a beach day memory fresh and crisp to the front of your mind. It's just as if you were right there again, with the sand between your toes, watching the tide come in. The feel of a certain texture of fabric—be it soft, smooth, or rough—can, when touched at the right moment, open the door to a memory that you thought you had left behind years ago. The unique taste of clam cakes and chowder, for me, always brings back memories of the old Rocky Point Amusement Park. As I said, some of my favorite childhood memories are anchored in that old park.

I find that, for most people, these memories can be quite pleasant. For me, these memories open doorways to the past that I truly can enjoy. That is, most of the time. Big exceptions are my memories of violence, which are triggered whenever I see the color red.

My formal introduction to violence in that household came at a very early age. I knew something was wrong with our family dynamic prior to the violence of that day, of course, but I did not know the reason behind it. I did not understand how my parents, the very people who were supposed to keep me safe from harm, could do these things. What I had just witnessed and experienced made no sense to my young mind, and it shook me to the core. I was just a kid, for god's sake.

My confusion about what happened that day still remains. Maybe parts of the memory were suppressed? I don't know. Forty-some-odd years later I still don't know why. I still don't understand what triggered the violence that day. (I suppose little children rarely do.) But little children should not have to see or go through the aftermath of what happened that day in the house of my childhood. Sadly, I was there, I was made to stay, and I bore silent witness to all that happened. My aversion to the color red started that day, and it is still with me now.

I remember parts of what happened that afternoon so clearly. It was a hot day. One of those godawful hot and humid days of late summer, the kind of day people call one of the dog days of August. Nary a breeze could be felt anywhere; not a single leaf was stirring in the trees. The humidity was so bad you felt that you could go outside and cut yourself a slice of air. God, was it so damned hot. "Lethargy" was the word of the day, lazing back somewhere trying to avoid the heat.

It was too hot to go outside that day, so I was indoors. I was playing with my Hot Wheels cars in the corner on the kitchen near the basement door. Lucille and my father were sitting at the kitchen table. Father was at the head of the table reading a newspaper. Lucille was sitting to the left of him, flipping through a magazine. The kitchen fans were the only relief from the heat in the house. On days like that, there is no escape from the high temperatures unless you have air conditioning. We did not.

The fan was one of those big, heavy, metal box fans everyone bought from Sears back then. It was painted silver and had a metallic protective grid on its front and back. It was running full speed, but making very little headway against the oppressive heat that it was trying to fight against. My oldest sister Lori, before she escaped the house, was sweeping the linoleum kitchen floor with an old straw broom—under protest, if I recall correctly. She was not happy about having to do it. I never remember Lori being happy in the house on Myra Road, either. She had such haunted eyes, and she always seemed a bit sad to me. There were always loud arguments between her and Lucille. The arguments were about how she was useless because she did not want to help Lucille by doing her chores. Father was always brought into the fights to administer Lucille's punishment of the day when he got home from work. One thing our stepmother learned about being a housewife in the seventies was once you had a child old enough to do the household chores, you never needed to do any housework ever again. She preferred to just sit back and punish her stepchildren severely until we learned to do it perfectly.

As Lori swept, I heard the sound of a small object hit the blades of the fan and shatter the oppressive silence. When that pebble hit that fan on that hot afternoon, the shit hit the fan as well. All hell broke loose in that heat-filled kitchen. It was a kitchen full of grumpy, miserable people on an ungodly hot day.

When that pebble hit the fan, things went from bad to worse. My father immediately accused Lori of sweeping dirt into the fan intentionally because she was angry at Lucille. I don't remember what was said next, but it eventually became a heated argument. I just knew my father was mad and it was a good time to work on my skills at becoming invisible. I was only four years old at this point, but even at four, I was already instilled with a healthy fear of our father's temper and his willingness to go straight to the belt for the most trivial of reasons. Years later, I recalled feeling glad that he was not angry with me, this time.

But all that changed with the sound of a solid *smack,* followed by my sister wailing in shock. I could not believe our father had hit her. I looked over to see Lucille telling her to go downstairs to her bedroom right away, and I looked up to see Lori run by me with streams of blood pouring down from her mouth and flowing onto the linoleum floor, creating small puddles. She struggled to get down into the basement without tripping over me. When she closed the door to the cellar, I stared at the red mess that covered the floor of the kitchen. Lucille just stood there with her hands on her hips, staring at all the blood, and pointed at our father, shouting, "Never in the face! I told you, never in the face!" I had no concept or understanding of what that meant for a long time, but I knew she was mad at our father for doing something wrong. I would have my own "Never in the face!" moment years later, and it was not until then that I really truly understood the meaning of what she said that day, when I was so young.

I can still remember the sound of a fist hitting flesh, which was instantly followed by the high-pitched wail of anguish from my sister as she ran downstairs to her room. And I can still hear that door slam shut. I was in shock. I just stood there, not knowing what to do. The song of my childhood resonates with my sister's mortified wailing. Another grain of sand on the pile.

Lucille retrieved a small, blue, Rubbermaid pail out from under the sink, as well as a small, fuzzy, blue facecloth that was the same color as the Cookie Monster puppet I loved so much. She filled the bucket with hot water and it looked at me like she was about to clean the blood off the floor. But my moment of invisibility that I used whenever adults were angry wore off, and she saw me, standing motionless, holding my Hot Wheels racecar in my hands. She handed the pail to me and told me not to spill it, and to get every last drop of my worthless sister's blood off the floor. If I did it wrong, I would go to bed without dinner that evening. So, with the exaggerated caution of a four-year-old, I knelt down and proceeded to clean up every speck of blood from the kitchen floor for what seemed to be an eternity. I remember being strangely proud of myself for doing such a good job, even with the confusing nature of what I was cleaning. As I went to dump the dirty water into the kitchen sink, Lucille asked me what I thought I was doing. I told her I had cleaned it all up. Then she asked me if I had done the stairs down into the basement, which had not occurred to me. Lucille changed the bucket water, put in more Octagon dish detergent, and sent me to clean the stairs to the cellar. I had to get the stairs done quickly, because they had just been carpeted and the blood might stain them if it dried too soon.

As a healthy four-year-old with a normal four-year-old's imagination, I lived in fear of the great cellar monster. It was not clear to me what he looked like or what he was, but I was quite sure he liked to eat little boys, or at least scare them to death. I knew my sister had a room down in the basement, but I assumed that her room was a safe place, and the monster could not get in there. (There was some weird illogical childhood reasoning mixed in there.) The one thing I was the most certain of is that you were the most vulnerable when you were on those stairs, going up or going down.

There were twelve steps leading down into the basement and all covered in that awful, seventies, print carpeting. At this moment, the project went from being a gross and unfair job to a very terrifying moment.

Step One

Clean step one. The memory of blood and red are now ingrained into my life. I can feel the cellar monster looking at me, biding its time.

Step Two

Clean step two. The memory of blood and red are now ingrained into my life. I want to run out of the basement screaming, but know I can't.

Step Three

Clean step three. The memory of blood and red are now ingrained into my life. I feel something brush my leg. I start to cry.

Step Four

    Clean step four. The memory of blood and red are now ingrained into my life. My stepmother opens the door and glares down the steps at me. She scares me more than the cellar monster, for a moment.

Step Five

    Clean step five. The memory of blood and red are now ingrained into my life. I hear a rapid pounding like something is running up the stairs to get me, but I realize it is only my heart.

Step Six

    Clean step six. The memory of blood and red are now ingrained into my life. My fear builds. I am so afraid.

Step Seven

    Clean step seven. The memory of blood and red are now ingrained into my life. I remember the cellar monster lives under the stairs and I have been on them for so long now. I am out of time.

Step Eight

    Clean step eight. The memory of blood and red are now ingrained into my life. A bead of sweat trickles down my back and I think it is the cellar monster running his finger down my spine. I scream.

Step Nine

    Clean step nine. The memory of blood and red are now ingrained into my life. I am sobbing because I know the cellar monster is going to get me at any moment now. I want it to be over.

Step Ten

    Clean step ten. The memory of blood and red are now ingrained into my life. I am so tired. Terror is exhausting, and I am almost out of tears.

Step Eleven

Clean step eleven. The memory of blood and red are now ingrained into my life. As I scrub the step, I have given into the eventuality of whatever fate my childish mind had created in the moment.

Step Twelve

Clean step twelve. The memory of blood and red are now ingrained into my life. The last step is done! I dash madly to the top of the stairs, convinced I will be snatched by the ankle as I try to step on the last step into the kitchen. I scream and jump two steps up to the kitchen floor, skipping over the last step to be safe. Triumph! I have evaded the monster. I have won this time.

This was my twelve-step program. The demon riding on my back was that cellar monster. I was terrified, I was shaking, but I had done it. I would learn there were worse things in the world than the cellar monster, and they were very, very real. Lori and I never spoke of what happened that day. It has been forty-plus years, and these memories of red still haunt me. The only person I have ever spoken to about this is my wife, and repeating the story aloud made it seem unreal, almost surrealistic. I felt I needed to write it down. I believe in karmic justice and that all sins are repaid out to those who commit them. I wonder to this day if the people who created these memories of mine even remember the events of that day, if they have lost one moment of sleep over what has haunted me for almost all my life.

In the years to follow, things would get much worse for all involved. But in my memory, this was the day the true horror started, the balance tipped, and my fate in that household was written. Monsters are real. Some people have to learn the hard way and then have to decide how to live with the knowledge for the rest of their lives. You can learn how to live; you can learn how to not let other people's bad decisions affect your life. But you cannot stop the dreams, the nightmares, or the memories. And they are always in red.

— 9 —

TOGETHER, ALONE

After many years of self-hatred, I came to an obvious but difficult conclusion: I was not to blame for what happened to me. The abuse had been part of Lucille's insidious plan all along. Her plan was to keep Lisa and me separated from each other and from the outside world as much as possible. My sister and I only had each other in that house, but we were not allowed to speak to one another. Alone together, we were never ever allowed a chance to get to know each other. Any form of bonding between the two of us was strictly forbidden. We would whisper to each other at the kitchen sink in stolen snatches of conversation while washing the dinner dishes, always afraid that Lucille would be lurking around the corner, eavesdropping. She was ever-present, making sure we did not ever break any of her insidious, lunatic fringe rules.

Lisa and I are doing the nightly routine of washing and drying the dishes tonight. We are quiet and dutiful, like good servants should be. The rest of the family is relaxing and watching television. As we stand side by side in front of the big double-sided stainless-steel sink, we whisper. One of us is washing, one of us is drying. We were making very sure every plate and glass, every piece of cutlery, and every pan is spotless, and every drop of water has been wiped off. There will be hell to pay if a spot of food is left on the edge of a plate, or a droplet of water should happen to leave a water mark on a glass.

Lisa and I are quietly talking to each other. There is no evil intent here, just a desire to talk to another sympathetic human being in the house. Lucille overhears us from the pantry where she has been lurking, trying to listen in on our conversation, attempting to catch us doing something wrong again—something truly punishment-worthy. Her paranoia takes over. She marches out of the pantry with her favorite weapon of household destruction: her oversized wooden spoon. Lucille stalks into the kitchen. She is glaring intently at the two of us. She begins to question us. Are we plotting against her with all our whispering? Are we making plans to, as she puts it, to make her life a living hell? After a thorough interrogation, the accusations of conspiracy have been debunked once more. Not guilty, your honor—this time, but the case is not closed. With prejudice, double jeopardy does not apply. She will continue to monitor us. Lucille then chuckles and says she thinks that Lisa and I must keep a secret calendar in the cellar with dates marked with whose day it is to ruin her life, and that we must have it planned out in advance.

I was old enough on that day to realize something was badly wrong with Lucille. Something was fundamentally broken inside of her, and there was nothing she could not justify doing to us. In her own mind, I believe she thinks she was being a good parent. Lisa and I made light of it after we were quite certain she had left, joking that we should really get a calendar and list whose day it was to torment

Lucille. Not that we would do it—we did not actually ever plot anything—but it was fun to joke about it that night. To joke about how unstable it made Lucille sound.

Never being trusted by my parents was always hurtful. To prevent me from stealing food, Lucille used to have me sing or whistle loud enough for her to hear. You can't eat if you are singing, right? In the wintertime, I would be sent down to do chores in the cellar. I had to sing loud enough so Lucille would know I was not getting into her food. If I was in any room where she could not see me, I would hear a shout of, "I don't hear you!" and I would start to sing once again, louder. I belted out classics of the day by Barry Manilow and Neil Diamond, and I whistled show tunes. I always felt like a trained talking parrot. *Polly want a cracker? No? Well David wants one, he is hungry.* Try to imagine having to sing or whistle to prove you are not a thief for eight consecutive hours, making noise so someone can keep track of where you are at all times. And all this in your own house, no less.

Another one of Lucille's favorite methods of punishment was duct tape. She would wrap it three times around our heads, covering our mouths. Once it was in place, we could not talk or eat, and we could only breathe through our noses. It was horribly claustrophobic. The duct tape was dually intended to maintain our silence as well. We could not tell relatives or neighbors what was wrong if our mouths were taped shut, now, could we?

Family reunions were an abject lesson on how people welcome clever lies over the awful truth. Lisa and I would walk about, taped up to the gills, like shackled slaves. Meanwhile, Lucille would sit back, holding court, telling everyone how badly we had behaved the day before. She would get uncomfortable nods of agreement about how bad we were, or blank unbelieving looks, that faded until the whole thing blew over.

Meme and Pepe in the back row
Middle row is Michael, Me, Dale Sr, Lisa and Monique is in the front

If the questions persisted, she explained to them that we were not being allowed to speak for an entire day as a punishment, then calmly invite everyone outside for a game of shuffleboard. We were shuttled out of view. She was so convincing that people did not want to believe what they thought they saw was real. So, they decided to accept this weak excuse, ignoring the obvious truth that was right in front of their faces. So many people saw what was going on but chose not to see it for what it was. The tape was allowed off to eat at the family reunions, but no talking was ever allowed while we were eating. When we were done, the tape went right back on. I hated the taste of duct tape. I hated the sticky mess the glue made on my skin. It's just a memory now, the days of duct tape and shame, but it still makes me want to scream out in frustration.

As I have said before, this abuse was all pre-planned. I would challenge anyone who tries to tell me any differently. If it was not planned, then why did we have clean, nice-looking clothes on hangers in the upstairs closet? The clothes were like neat little stage props. We could not wear them unless the director told us to for a scene. These were the clothes that we were only allowed to wear if social services or the Department of Children and Families (DCF) called to say they had received a complaint and were going to make a visit. Why did we each have a bed in the upstairs bedrooms with nice clean sheets, yet they were beds we were not even allowed to sit on? We were told to let people believe that was where we normally slept. We were threatened with dire punishments if we spoke a word of the truth to anyone checking up on us, because after all, they would have to leave sometime. They always left.

"No evidence of abuse here. Wow, your neighbor must really have it in for you to have called in a complaint like this."

Then, once the social worker had left, we would be Lucille's again to do with as she wished. The interrogation would begin soon thereafter. *Had we had the nerve to complain to someone? Why did they come? What did we do? Who did we tell? Which one of you broke the rules?* Over and over with the questions, making us feel more and more afraid. What the social workers did not see was worse than any of them could have imagined. I was locked into the lie. I played my role to perfection. I was the normal-dressed, normal kid, with a normal room and a normal bed. Nothing to see here. Move on, please move on, because I am so afraid of the woman standing behind you, glaring at me. My choice is to comply with Lucille's demands or face a sadistic punishment.

What many people fail to understand is that when you live in fear every day and every night, in your dreams and in your nightmares, there is never peace. There is no calm in the middle of the storm. There is no hope or joy, just fear—a rotting fear of those who are supposed to take care of you, love you, and nurture you. It might have been their intention, at one point in the beginning, to be a loving father, a loving mother, or a loving stepmother; however, the reality was otherwise. Somewhere along the line, paranoia and jealousy reared their ugly heads and commanded the scene.

Lucille's twin children, Michael and Monique, were children of her own blood and body and were all she cared about in our family. The twins were destined to be the premier members of the household, the special children, the chosen ones, our family's version of Cinderella's stepsisters. But for us, there was no glass slipper, no magical clothing, no enchanted pumpkin carriage, and most of all, no Disney prince or princess to ride into our rescue at the end of the story. Because for us, there was no potential for a happily ever after. All we saw in our futures was more of the same: fear, abuse, hunger, forced feeding, beatings. These were our reality, and there was no escape that we could see. We were locked in a jail fashioned by our own minds, after years of systematic abuse, and our parents held the keys. Just one single glance from Lucille would freeze my blood, turning me into a gibbering mass that would do anything to please her and make her move on and leave me alone, at least for a short while.

— 10 —

CLOTHES ARE A PRIVILEGE

One of a child's most basic needs is clothing. Parents have the responsibility to provide good clothing for their children. Making sure that a child's clothing is neat and presentable is simple parenting. All of us need to have clothes, if only just for environmental issues and for modesty's sake. Replacement clothing is normally provided as you outgrow what you have or wear things out. School clothes for the new school year, such as sneakers, shoes, gym clothes, and jackets are all things a child needs while they are growing up. Larger families might have hand-me-downs—used, but serviceable clothes that an older sibling wore until they outgrew them. They may be pre-used, but they still have a usable life left in them. Starting the new school year with at least one or two new outfits to wear is common practice as well, in most families. Retailers hold back-to-school sales every year to take advantage of this very thing. Moms march through the shops with a strict look of determination on their faces. Their dutiful children trudge close behind with the knowledge that summer is almost over and school will be starting soon. Mom rummages through the clothing racks to pick out the perfect outfits for her kids. Then comes the inevitable fashion show near the fitting rooms. Children model the new clothes as their mother picks what fits, what looks good, what to keep, and what to put back on the racks. This is normal behavior that is expected of most parents—clothe your children with something better than shredded rags. No, name brands are not required here—just good, serviceable shirts, pants, and shoes to wear throughout the year.

I remember having new school clothes just like these when we lived at Myra Road. We resided in a tight-knit little neighborhood, and everyone knew each other. Because we were in such close proximity to prying eyes, everyone had to look perfect all the time. My father and Lucille were close acquaintants with many of the neighbors in this very closely placed block of houses. There was no way to keep secrets there, and the appearance of normalcy had to be maintained at all costs.

The quality of my clothes and Lisa's clothes deteriorated quickly once we arrived in West Greenwich. To be honest, I was oblivious to the changes at first. I was just a kid. This kid wanted a new G.I. Joe, a Stretch Armstrong action figure, and a new bike, not a new shirt and a pair of jeans. I did not care about my clothing in the slightest. It covered me, it kept me warm, and protected as it was supposed to, I guess. But honestly, what boy cares about the specifics of his clothes when he is young? By the time I started to notice, it was too late. I was too young to do anything about it, and I was too enveloped in fear to question why.

As it was with many families at the time in my youth, there were two times of the year where children normally received clothes: back to school, and Christmas. I think every kid hates to open Christmas presents knowing there are clothes inside. You need those clothes, of course, but you are disappointed just the same. You sit down and dutifully open the present from Meme and Pepe. Then you put on what you hope is a grateful looking smile the whole time and offer a polite *thank you* for the underwear. I hated those rectangular boxes that always signified the gift of clothing...that is, until I didn't.

When I was about nine or ten, my clothing started to change noticeably. This change was happening to Lisa as well. We received nothing new and our clothes were not allowed to be washed. And to put it bluntly, we stunk.

We were also not allowed to bathe. Early on we bathed once a month; later, for me, it became once every three months. The only clean clothes we owned were the "special" outfits that Lucille had put aside for when company was over. We were also allowed to bathe so we would be clean for any special occasions with the relatives. On those days, we had to act like there was nothing wrong with our lives. We were told plainly that if we talked to anyone about our living situation, we would never speak to anyone again. We believed it. So, we never spoke of these things and I lived in constant fear of my own murder. This was very real to me and had the added benefit of feeding my nightmares as I slept.

On the rare occasion that Lisa and I were allowed to bathe, we were always fifth and sixth in line for the bath water. Filthy bath water was all we ever got to use. Lucille said she did not believe in wasting water, so we all had to share it. First in got out clean, last in got out still dirty from that brown, disgusting water. Then we got to dry off with towels that have been used six times before us. When we were finished, we had to step back into our stinking, unwashed clothes. I did not feel clean for over eight years.

Today is a laundry day. I run the washers and dryers, washing Lucille, Dale, Monique, and Michael's piles and piles of dirty clothes. Then comes the really fun part—I get to fold and iron it all, even though none of my own rags are among them. The folding must be up to Lucille's exacting standards, the ironing must be perfect—no burn marks, no missed or ironed-in wrinkles. They each have so much clothing. I cannot comprehend having that much clothing to wear. The wood-burning furnace is fifteen feet behind me and is blazing away. Sweat pours off me. I gag on the smell of myself. Carefully, I keep my hands clean to touch the others' laundry, because there are consequences if I leave traces of myself. I have four outfits total that I am allowed to wear around the house and to school. They are fragrant with the cloying smell of my unwashed body. I can even taste the smell of my dirty clothes from ten feet away, ripe, rotting, knowing they are mine. I am not allowed to wash them for another three months. Every day I try to choose the lesser of evils; I do a sniff test to see which set of clothes stinks less today. As I get dressed to start the day, I once again resist the urge to vomit. I am fourteen years old; I stink and I live in constant despair of my continued existence. As I stand there doing others' laundry, not being allowed to wash my own, I wish I could fade away...disappear.

A year before high school started, my clothing problems reached an all-new low. One of Lucille's friends gave her a large bag of women's clothing straight out of the early seventies. The bag included polyester, side-zip pants and women's floral blouses, all of them horribly out of style but still serviceable for a young lady with no other choice. Much to my dismay, Lucille had me try them on, and—oh, joy of joys—they fit. A new die was cast. I got four outfits from that god-awful bag, and they were the only ones I would wear for the next three years, with the exception of my father's company outings, baseball games, and school picture day. Because I was so repellant, I had zero friends. Who would want to talk to me? Getting too close made people nauseous. Why should they bother?

As I have stated before, Lisa and I were only allowed to wash our clothes once every three months. We had a rotting wooden box in the basement where we had to keep our clothes, separate from everyone else's. Our clothes were not allowed to come into contact with any real people's clothes. Heaven forbid our clothes touched and sullied a human's clothes—there would be hell to pay. The rotting box of clothes was just to the right of the washing machine and the dryer. Lisa and I were required to do all the laundry for the house, but were not allowed to do our own. We had to wash it, hang it on the lines to dry, take it down, and spend all laundry day in the acrid basement, ironing and folding the massive amount of new and fashionable items the rest of the house members got to wear.

In my old closet upstairs was my one good outfit. It was the "for special occasions" outfit, kept on hand for when the state came calling or for school picture day so we could keep up the appearance that we were a normal family.

Try to imagine yourself wearing the same four outfits for three months. They do not get washed and you do not get to bathe, yet you spend all day outside in the heat, working chores around the property. Your clothes are starting to literally rot on your body, but you cannot let Lucille find out because she will accuse you of trying to intentionally ruin your clothes to get new ones. Eventually your nose goes numb to the smell and you no longer notice it—that is, until you see the faces of the people around you, and the reaction they have to you as you walk by. This kind of treatment kills your soul and makes you feel less than human, but you must go on. After all, today might be the day you finally get to die.

— 11 —

SCHOOL DAYS

In my early years of attending school, I had several developmental issues to deal with. These developmental issues continued for most of my middle school years, too. I was, to put it mildly, writing and spelling challenged. I could not hold a pencil in my hand to write. I could not grip it tight enough. The issue was a physical developmental issue that is called pencil grip. The teachers had me wear a lovely brace that had a metal holder to keep the pencil in the proper position for me. The pencil that went with the brace was over half an inch thick so my fingers could grip it tightly enough to write. I was not fond of this device because it made me look and feel different from the other kids in my class. Compounding my limitations with the use of a pencil was my spelling. I frequently spelled my own name wrong, along with most of the rest of what I had written. My fourth-grade teacher, Mrs. Couples, took note of my problems and sat with me to try to help me improve my penmanship and spelling. These were subjects that you were graded on at that time, and she was concerned I might have to be held back if I could not improve.

Mrs. Couples started by making me read out loud to her from a book. It did not go well. After that debacle, she had me write short stories for her that I had to read aloud. After this was done, she noticed I could read my own writing, as bad as it was, with ease. However, I was barely able to read aloud from a book because I always got the words wrong. The next day one of the school's therapists came and got me from class to run some tests. The tests dealt with my reading and writing skills and how I perceived the written word. She very quickly confirmed what Mrs. Couples had suspected: I was dyslexic. A parent-teacher meeting was immediately scheduled to let Lucille and my father know what my reading issue was and how to help me with it. I did not understand the technical aspect of my disability (I was too young to grasp such a concept); I just knew my mind saw things differently than normal people did.

The school staff wanted to help me fix it, and this was a good thing. I did not like being different from the other kids in my class. Being different at that age can quite often be less than fun. Kids can be cruel to anyone who is different; it's just a part of growing up. I desperately wanted to stop being different and fit in. I was optimistic that they could help me be a normal kid, and all the insufferable teasing would end.

Lucille and I went in for the meeting about my reading problems with Mrs. Couples. It was explained to Lucille that I had a learning disability called dyslexia. Lucille replied that she had always thought I was retarded and asked if I was going to be sent to special ed classes from then on. Lucille was told that no, I was not stupid or retarded, just learning impaired. I had a common learning disability that could be fixed and managed over time. Mrs. Couples explained to Lucille in detail what was needed to start helping me read and write better. I don't remember the details, to be honest, but I do remember one part quite clearly: Mrs. Couples told Lucille that it would be extremely helpful to my disability if I was given a typewriter to use at home. This would allow me to type my homework assignments and keep up with the class. She then told Mrs. Couples that it was pointless to get me a typewriter because I would only just destroy it. She went on to explain to Mrs. Couples I broke everything I touched, and it would just be a waste of money. The meeting eventually ended as these types of meetings always did—I went home with Lucille, and nothing was done about the issue. The only thing that changed was that Lucille now had more ammunition to make me feel stupid. That evening at the dinner table she spoke to my father about getting Monique a typewriter because, after thinking about it, she felt she could really use one. They purchased an electric typewriter secondhand shortly after that, but I was never allowed to touch it.

Over the next few years, with the help of the school staff and my burgeoning swamp Yankee stubbornness, I finally managed to overcome and manage my dyslexia. My hand also got stronger, so I was able to hold a normal pencil without a brace. But I never did become one of the normal kids like I had desired. Lucille had already started her sadistic campaign of abuse in my life, and it played out in school, too. Ratty, hand-me-down clothes that stunk had become the normal for me. Now add a lovely bowl haircut with jagged, uneven bangs that would become my signature look for years to come.

Despite my early problems with dyslexia—or maybe even because of it—I learned I loved to read. Books became some of my best friends. *Tom Swift, The Hardy Boys, The Hobbit, The Dragon Riders of Pern...* books like these helped me get through some of the darkest parts of my youth. They were a rare escape from my awful world.

Of course, when Lucille discovered this, I lost the privilege of books. I was no longer allowed to read them when I was in the house. My schoolbooks would be placed at the door when I got home each day. I would not be allowed to touch them until I had to get ready to leave the house the next morning. No homework could be done. I would try to get it done on the bus ride to school, but the ride was not ever long enough. I frequently missed homework assignments.

On parent teacher night, I would have to sit there and listen to

Lucille talk about how I was lazy and mentally challenged. I would listen to her say how she thought I was retarded, and that she wanted me placed in special education classes. Yes, of course she gave me time every day for me to do homework—I was just too stupid to do it. Once again, Lucille was able to sell the same old story, and most of the teachers bought it. The power of denial is a strong force. People want to believe any explanation they are told. A good lie is easier to believe than a harsh truth. Lucille tried to get Lisa placed in special education, as well. I am so glad that the teachers, at least, did not buy into that part of the lie.

———

I am eleven years old. I woke up this morning feeling very sick. I have a cough and can't breathe all that well. I do not know what is wrong with me but asking to stay home is out of the question. It is not smart to be the only child home with Lucille. It draws her attention to you and that is never, ever a good thing.

So, I suck it up and ride the bus into school. Very shortly after I arrive, I begin to feel worse and worse, and I am eventually sent to the nurses' office by my teacher, Mrs. Brown, because she says I am burning up. It turns out I have a fever of 102.9°F (39.38°C), and the nurse says that I should go to the emergency room because I might have whatever bug has been going around the school. She then calls my home; Lucille is not there but it happens to be my father's day off from work, so he comes to get me. The nurse tells him I need the ER and that I am one sick little boy. He signs me out for the day, and we drive off in his beat-up old Ford van. I notice we are going straight home and not to see the doctor. I ask him why, and he says he was working on something at home; when it is done, we can go to the ER. This seems reasonable to me, so I ride quietly the rest of the way home with him.

Once we get home, I find out he has been working down in the cellar putting mortar in the cracks in the stone walls around the fireplace. He has also started to replace some of the cement inside the fireplace as well. He is trying to get as far up into the chimney flue as his arms can reach. Meanwhile, all I can do is sit and watch him work.

At this point in my life, there just does not seem to be anything that my father cannot fix around the house with his own hands and his trusty tool set. Even after all these years of punishments, I still love my dad. I am deathly afraid of him, but I love him just the same. He taught me how to play catch and how to hit a baseball. Basically, everything I knew about baseball I learned from him.

As he works in the chimney flue, he gets to a point where he can no longer reach with the trowel to finish the repair. Now comes the fun part of my family time with Dad today. He looks at me and decides that I would be the perfect solution to his problem. So, he has me crawl into the fireplace, then climb up inside the chimney flue—which is a tight fit, even for me at that age. The flue is literally full of centuries of soot and mortar dust that stirs up every time I move. I start to cough so much I can barely breathe. He then holds me by my feet and pushes me further up into the chimney. He has me use a trowel and mortar to patch things up as far as I can reach. It is suffocating. After he can't push me any higher, he has me climb up alone as high as I can, bracing in the tight flue to patch the mortar as far up as I can.

Spoiler Alert: this does not help my fever. This, in fact, makes it worse. I never did make it to the ER that day, but I did get to cement a lasting, twisted memory of time spent with my father.

— 12 —

PLAYING CHARADES

After our family moved to Kitt's Tavern on Weaver Hill Road, our Christmases transformed into something disturbingly twisted. A game of deprivation had now been put into play. The constant lack of amenities and the withholding of basic human comforts had become weaponized for use against my father's children. Deprivation is a very slow and subtle form of torture. When done in small increments, it bleeds you dry before you even notice it. Eventually you become accustomed to getting less, being treated like less, and it becomes your accepted norm. It is as it has always been—being deprived, abused, neglected, unloved, unwanted—all of this, and more. This was just a normal day in the life of the Harter children.

At Kitt's Tavern, the Christmas season became the ultimate exercise in deprivation. It was a blunt emotional weapon designed to show us how little we mattered. We were being trained to stay in our place. We were not wanted nor needed there. We were just the unpaid labor force, and servants dare not complain. We would have presents under the tree every year, because there had to be something there for us to open for appearance's sake—Meme and Pepe would be there. The appearance of normalcy had to be kept up; our lives could not be allowed to become suspicious. There was always one big present for Lisa and me to open, a special present so Lucille could prove, "Look! They are treated normally in this house. See?" Most of our presents came from Meme and Pepe of course—things like underwear, socks, or a new shirt or two maybe. Practical items, every one of them. I would desperately play with my big toy all day, in between the food and family socializing. I knew that, within a day or two, Lucille would take my new, shiny toy away from me with some twisted use of her sadistic logic. Up in the attic the new gift would go, stowed away with all the other forgotten toys of years past. These were toys that, having served their purpose as a tool of deception, would now gather dust and never be played with again.

As for the new clothing that we received from Meme and Pepe, well, Lucille put those to good use, too. Those clothes would become our new "special" outfits destined to hang in the upstairs closet with care, waiting to be worn on those days when we had to look normal for the world to see. There could be no appearance of impropriety or neglect on display to be seen by anyone who might start asking questions. So, we dressed nice, and performed our perfect performance of happiness. And when the show was over, we put the props away till they were needed for the next performance piece, another tableau for the DCF or surprise visitors.

This was Christmas to us: put on a happy face, dress up in our special clothes, eat good food, and feel normal—for a few hours, that is. Then, the good times would always end and it was all back to the same old, same old. Time to pack away the smiles, stash away the pretty lies until they were needed again, and get back to our real place in that house: back to work. For that short time on Christmas day, however, we became part of Lucille's decorations. God help us if we made a mistake or gave the family secrets away. We always stuck to the script; we had no choice in this. *We were one big perfect happy family, see?* No one could know what was really going on inside those walls. Life might have been a living hell for us, but I learned that the temperature in hell can get worse by degrees of intensity. Lucille had her hand poised over the thermostat of our lives, watching our every action. Christmas was the one day out of the year where we got to see what happy looks like, and I learned to dread its coming every year.

Living with constant deception and lies is like trying to play charades with no hands. This was my life inside Kitt's Tavern. We had so many habits drilled into us that helped Lucille keep the whole house of cards from collapsing in on her. There were so many pretty, little lies. I lied to my teachers—*I am fine, look away, nothing to see here. Please don't notice; she will be so angry if you notice.* I lied to everyone outside of our house. I lied so much about what was happening in that house that it became my own personal truth. I even started to believe them. But the worst lies were the ones that we had to tell to make our own serial abuser feel validated in the world. Those were the worst rituals of all.

Ah. The ritual of the goodnight kiss. The act of kissing your lovely parents goodnight while telling them you love them. This is a heartwarming and loving nightly ritual in many houses all around the world. This is a loving act, to always make sure you go to bed with "I love you" on your lips. There are no guarantees in this world; bad things can happen at any moment. Make sure the last thing you say to a loved one is that you love them, and always, always say goodbye. Life is too short for regrets. In the house on Weaver Hill, we had a similar, if somewhat more perverse ritual. Lucille's nightly ritual of self-validation reenforced her twisted control over us, one kiss and one "I love you" at a time.

Looking back now, what we endured in that house seems so surreal. The humiliation of it all still breaks my heart. Lucille had her own twisted, personal version of ritual of the goodnight kiss. The ritual went something like this: first, line up in a queue to give Lucille a kiss on the cheek. Then tell her enthusiastically that we loved her. And it was done always with our father standing vigil beside her, watching carefully for infractions of the house rules. We had to look happy; no eye rolling or unhappy, sullen looks were allowed here. Once again, there was no option but to comply with a happy mask as required. What also was required was to say a genuine and heartfelt "I love you," and God help you if Lucille did not feel it sounded genuine enough. You have to keep trying to be sincere, to eventually convince Lucille of your undying love for her. But our failure to get the ritual of the kiss correct on the first attempt would result in something very, very bad. It did not matter how horrible our day had been. It did not matter how cruel and vindictive Lucille might have been to us just moments before. We would pay dearly for this particular transgression later. We would wake up the next morning with the fear of impending doom, waiting for the other shoe to drop—and it always did, with authority. Lucille never forgot nor forgave anything we did that she felt jilted her or her perfect household.

In the beginning, before our world turned to ashes in our mouth, the goodnight kiss was likely genuine. But with the passing of the years, and the increasing levels of abuse that were piled on top of Lisa and me, that kiss transformed into just another subtle form of abuse. Who wants to kiss their abuser and be forced to tell them how much you love them? How many forced, shallow, and empty goodnight kisses, how many hollow refrains did we give over to Lucille over the years? How many times did we utter a painful, "I love you"? The very words "I love you" were the words that we grudgingly performed with a complete and total lack of conviction every night. We had to have our smiles painted on, always with a happy face. We were thespians in the seemingly endless drama that was our existence.

I lack the drive or the desire to tabulate the sum total of emotional damage done by the events of my childhood. Yet I do know one thing: despite all the countless times that we gave voice to the words "I love you," they fell into an empty void. Neither Lisa nor I can ever recall Lucille or our father ever saying that they loved us back. Not once, not ever. Oh, we said "I love you" to her every night, but her reply was always, "You too," never "I love you too," or "I love you." It was just another empty vessel to carry us through till the next night's ritualistic goodnight kiss. We grew up in an emotional desert, devoid of affection of any kind. We were always on the outside looking in. We wanted to belong, we truly did, and we tried, every day, to earn Lucille's love. But Lucille had no love to give us. There was no love to spare for a child that was not hers by blood.

We were just children, for god's sake. We were innocent. We knew nothing of the world. We did not know what was normal and what was broken. We did not know why our family was so badly broken, but broken it was. There wasn't a damned thing we could have done about it back then. Seeing it now, with hindsight, it seems so obvious to me. We did nothing wrong. The game was rigged, the deck of life was stacked, there was no way to win the game. It is simplicity itself to see now what was wrong in our lives, because hindsight is easy. But back then, after all the carefully planned and executed years of abuse, we truly thought we were doing something wrong. I thought that I was the one who was broken, and I tried so very hard to fix myself and make Lucille love me, even though I didn't appreciate that she never would or could. We didn't know any better. This was the family we were born into, and to us, this was normal.

— 13 —

THE LONG COLD WALK

I am eight years old, and I currently attend the fourth grade in Mrs. Couples's class at Wawaloam Elementary School in Exeter, Rhode Island. It is a seven-mile bus ride to the school. We ride to school on bus number twelve with Mrs. Bruno, our driver. She picks us up and drops us off every day.

On this cold day in January, Lucille has me do some odd chore just before the bus is due to arrive. I believe I had to bring out the garbage to the fifty-five-gallon drums that we use as storage bins in the backyard. She is yelling at me to hurry and get it done in time for school, and that I had better not miss the bus. Ultimately, I did run out of time. The bus comes and goes, and I am not on it. I can see the bus the whole time, and I am running down the driveway in vain, trying to catch up to it. I watch in horror as the doors close, and the bus drives away.

I realize I am now in deep trouble and sit out in the breezeway for a few minutes. I am so afraid to tell Lucille that I missed the bus. I finally get up the nerve to go back into the house; Lucille sees me and flips out. She says that I missed the bus on purpose to spite her, and there is absolutely no way that she is going to drive me all the way to school. I assume that I will be punished and have to stay home and do added work around the house all day. But I was wrong…so very wrong.

Lucille decides she is going to teach me a lesson. She tells me I am going to walk all the way to school, all seven miles, at the ripe age of eight years old, by myself, on a frigid January morning. I have no concept of the distance, but I do know that it is a very, very long walk. So, I put on my winter hat and zip up my jacket. I look everywhere, but I cannot find my gloves. Lucille says to forget them, and that I had better get out there and start walking now, because I am already late for school. She also tells me that I am not allowed to take a ride from anyone, even if I know and trust them. I know that to talk back would make matters far worse, so I keep my mouth closed, go out the breezeway door, and head down the driveway to start my long, cold walk to school.

At this age, I do not know what it means to "gird your loins," but for me, it was easy to gather the intestinal fortitude to do an unpleasant task. It was something I was already well acquainted with. So, I walked out of our driveway and started my walk down Weaver Hill Road. To do this walk, you need to go about three-quarters of a mile to the end of the road we live on, then underneath an overpass where interstate Route 95 passes overhead. Then you take a right onto State Route 3, Nooseneck Hill Road, and walk a few miles all the way down to Route 102 Victory Highway, where it heads southeast into the neighboring town of Exeter.

So, as I am walking down the road, Lucille drives slowly past me in the family's AMC Hornet and waits for me, with the car idling ahead at the overpass. I am starting to feel truly cold, so when I get to the car, I am relieved and I open the door to get in. I assume at this point, in my naïve way, that Lucille thinks I have learned my lesson, and that I will get to ride in the car the rest of the way to school. As I stand there with the wonderful warming wave of heat pouring out of that open car door, I am informed by Lucille she will be riding ahead of me in the car to make sure no one attempts to give me a ride to school and ruin her punishment.

I shut the door of the car, sealing all that wonderful heat away from me, and the bitter January cold immediately starts to soak into me once again. She drives up the road for a bit. Then I see the brake lights turn on as she pulls over, with the car still running, waiting for me to catch up. I longingly look at the exhaust coming from the car and am jealous of the heat it represents. I am upset. I am a child. So, I do what a cold, upset child does. I start to cry. Crying is just a part of life for me now. I feel no shame in it anymore. "Big boys don't cry" is a mantra for boys of my generation, but it does not apply to me. I am cold and I think that the whole world hates me. How can it not hate me if this is happening to me right now? The problem with crying in this situation is my tears. They start to freeze, leaving tracks of ice in my eyelashes and down my face, and freezing on my coat. This scares me. It is so cold. So, I start to cry even harder. I cannot stop crying. I discover another complication from crying in the January cold: a runny nose. Soon I have an icicle of snot hanging off one nostril. I was wiping my nose off at the start, but the skin got too raw and it just hurt too much to wipe it off anymore. I give in to the inevitable and simply leave it alone.

I cannot stop crying as this torture continues for the next two to three hours. I catch up with the car. Lucille drives ahead. I catch up with the car. Lucille drives ahead. For my entire seven-mile walk, she repeats this cruel game over and over again. She pulls forward about one-quarter of a mile at a time so she won't lose sight of me. My hands are so cold they have stopped hurting. They are numb. I can no longer feel my toes, either. My face feels as if it is frozen in place, yet still, I walk on. To stop is just unthinkable to me. If I do not do this, Lucille will simply find another way to punish me even worse. I keep walking…crying…freezing. I am a zombie trudging on, one foot in front of the other. All I want is the feeling of warmth against my skin once more.

Eventually, several hours later, I shamble into the lobby of the school and Lucille drives away. I walk into Mrs. Couples's room; she takes one look at me and her jaw hits the floor. She runs over to see if I am okay. I am most definitely not okay. I have a streamer of frozen snot attached to my nose and my face is covered in frozen tears. I am a mess, to say the least. Then real pain begins as my fingers and toes start to thaw out. The pain is so horrible I start to sob out loud, wanting to scream but not doing so out of shame. I am now crying in front of my classmates. Some giggle and some look away. I know they will not forget it. Children never forget when others show weakness. I am sent to the nurses' office because Mrs. Couples is worried I might have frostbite. Fortunately, I just need a bit of a thaw and some rest, then I am sent back to class with a clean bill of health.

Then the unavoidable wave of questions come at me. How did I get in the condition I was in? It was my fault, I tell them. Why did I walk to school in the cold? Because I was bad and missed the bus, I tell them. Why did I not get a ride to school from my parents? I tell them I chose to walk to school because I was bad. Why was I not wearing gloves? Because I forgot them of course. I make mistakes a lot.

The thought of hanging Lucille out to dry was not an option. If Lucille was to be held accountable for her actions, the school staff would have to make the first move. They knew something horrible was going on but felt powerless to help. And I would not tell, because at some point I would have to go home. At some point I would have to face her again, and I want to eat, and be warm, and I am so afraid of her. After today, I am more afraid of her than I have ever been before. The staff at the school tries to get me to talk to them about what happened. Again. I will not break. I will not give in. I will never tell. Telling might help me at first, but I still had to go home to HER, and home to HIM, and that was so much worse than anything they could conceive or understand. In no world could I tell them all that was really happening and escape from that house. Game, set, match, Lucille. I believe, deep down in my eight-year-old mind, that I can never win.

— 14 —

MY BROTHER'S KEEPER

For years I held a dirty, shameful secret. In fact it was a huge secret. I could not tell anyone. No one would have believed me anyway, and there would have been hell to pay if I told. Somehow, in some way, this would all have been my fault. In my world at Kitt's Tavern, it always is.

―――

Michael is a asking me...no, making me let him do something secret, something bad and dirty that feels strange to me. I do not understand his actions. I do not like what he wants to do. Why does he want to lay on top of me and rub his penis against my bum? I tell him no; I do not want to. He threatens to break something and tell Lucille that I did it, knowing I will get punished badly for it. I know this is not a hollow threat. He has done this before, and no one believed me last time. I remembered the strappings, beatings, and various other tortures I had endured as a result of his lies. I have to consider his request, but I still am afraid of what he wants to do to me. He offers to give me his blue, rubber shark toy that I love so much. He says if I let him do it, I can have the shark toy. With no real choice, I eventually give in, and he takes out his penis and puts it against my bum, and then he starts rubbing it up and down against me. What the heck is he doing? This feels weird, wrong, and gross. Then he starts to breathe hard, and he gets this hot, sticky, messy stuff all over my bum and back. I am freaked out. Then he wipes me off and gives me the rubber shark toy and goes back to his bed.

The next morning, he gets up and acts like nothing is wrong, but he immediately runs off to tell Lucille that I had stolen his shark toy. She comes storming into the room, lifts my blanket, and finds the shark. I am guilty, caught in the act. My punishment for this infraction is no breakfast or lunch, plus a list of chores to do in the gardens and around the property. And if I don't finish the list to Lucille's satisfaction, there will be no supper as well. I also get to look forward to Dad coming home and the beating I will get from him. I take all my punishments. I still do not know what Michael had done to me, but it felt wrong and I wanted no one to know about it. Even if I wanted to tell someone, who would believe me? Michael could do no wrong, and I was just a horrid, little, lying child. He would deny the act anyway, and I would just face more punishment.

A week later, he wants to do it again. No children's toys are offered this time, just a threat that if I say no, the punishment I received the week before will seem like nothing. He has the same twisted smirk on his face that Lucille gets when she knows she has you, and there is nothing you can do about it. So, shamefully, I let him do it again. Week after week, this pattern repeats. The threats changed from time to time, but the shame was always the same.

One morning, he wanted to do it just before school. Lisa and Monique walked into the room and caught us in the act. I was horrified, and to be honest, so were my sisters. From their expressions I could tell they were not sure what they saw, but I am sure they had a pretty good idea. I think I might have been the only one in the room that morning who did not at least have an inkling of an idea of what sex was. After this incident, Michael becomes more cautious, making me come with him to more private spots. The clubhouse shed is a favorite, as is the basement couch, in the woods, and, quite frankly, anywhere he thought he could get away with it.

This became an almost weekly event until I escaped that place, years later. His attentions became more adult and more painful over time, but it was just another indignity in life as I knew it. I look at the last four paragraphs I just wrote, and I marvel that something that has had such a dramatic impact on my life fits into four short paragraphs. It seems so small a thing when I look at it that way. But in fact, it has impacted my entire life. How sexual assault was viewed when this was happening to me—and for several decades after, as a matter of fact—was different than it is today. There is less shame and victim-blaming today than there was forty years ago. When I was the victim of sexual assault, it was shameful, mortifying, and no one spoke of it. It just was not done—suffer in silence, toe the line, be a man, suck it up. And if you let it happen, you must be secretly gay because no man allows himself to be sexually assaulted.

For years, I questioned my sexuality because of this. I am heterosexual, I am certain, but from time to time these assaults pop in for a quick visit on memory lane, and I begin to question myself all over again. As for my opinion on sexuality, I don't care who you love; just make sure you love him or her with all your heart. I do not care who you make love to, just be an attentive, caring lover. Love always, with all your heart, and never be afraid to fall, because in falling we learn to live and love again.

The pitfall of being a male sexual assault survivor is the shame, an overpowering shame that just never seems to want to go away. It takes up residence in your mind and it lives there rent-free for years, popping up like an unwanted visitor when you least expect it, wreaking havoc in your life. It forces you to relive those moments all over again and makes you question yourself again, and again, and again.

My sister Lisa and I have shared the experiences of these assaults many times with each other over the years. I do not know how many times she was sexually assaulted; some things are best left unspoken, and I will not ask. I just know of the one time I heard them in our parents' room. I could tell they were on the floor and the doors were locked. I heard her crying, and I heard him ordering her around just like he did to me as she cried, "Ow, ow, ow, please stop!" But he ignored her, and he ignored my tapping on the door. I was not even supposed to be upstairs; Lucille was out doing errands, and I was supposed to be outside doing chores. I had snuck into the house for some reason that I don't remember. I knew if I got caught in the house there would be hell to pay. I ran back out of the house and tried to forget what I had just heard. There was no point in telling. No one in that house would have believed my word, or Lisa's word, over Michael's.

Basically, what I am saying is that our parents would not have believed us. The house we lived in was not conducive to anyone believing us, even if we told the truth. We had been conditioned by so many years of abuse and deprivations not to speak to anyone outside of the household, so that was never an option in our minds. This twisted situation allowed our stepbrother to start his own little sexual assault club, in his own household, because he knew that no one would report his actions to anyone.

These acts of assault were performed by a minor, so there will be no justice for Lisa or me. There never has been nor will there ever be justice for us—for any of it, for that matter. These assaults were the acts of a dangerous predator. These perverse actions eventually became more aggressive as we got older. It went from rubbing his penis in between my butt cheeks and spending himself onto my back to much worse. At least once a week for over three years, he sexually assaulted me. He was relentless. I remember the pain, the humiliation, and the shame of it all. For years, I was so sexually confused. I did not like it, but I had allowed it to happen. Did that make me gay? I had no attraction to men, ever, but I had allowed this, so what did that mean? I know now who and what I am, but that took years of uncertainty and pain to figure out.

— 15 —

BEHIND THE CELLAR DOOR

The cellar door is locked again.
Once again, they have turned out the lights.
Why?
What have I done?
What did I do?
I am alone.
In the dark.
I am afraid.
Of the dark.
Why do you not love me?
What have I done wrong?
In the darkness, I hear the vermin scurry on their way.

―――

How can I find the words to make you understand the horror of this part of my narrative? How do I explain the deep, primal fear that these memories can still evoke in me to this day? What words can I use to convey to you, the reader, just how dreadful it was? How do I suspend your disbelief? I have come upon a part of my narrative that, even though it is based on the truth, people might still think it is a work of fiction. Even though these things really happened to me, I will still have to deal with the barrier of plausible deniability. Some people will read this, look up, and shake their heads in denial, thinking that there is no way, no chance, that this could have happened in the real world, in the 20th century, in America.

I actually have discovered something about myself while writing this book: I no longer care if I am believed or not. Belief in my narrative is not relevant at this point. This narrative is about letting go. Letting go of the anger and the baggage of forty years of nightmares. If I offend someone with what I say here, I am truly sorry. However, I challenge them to think what it might be like to live through this. This is my story; it really did happen. Disbelief will not change the fact that I did go through this living hell and still deal with it every day. For me, the act of writing this is a release. It's my own way of coping with the demons of my past. It is my way of coping with my memories of that cellar, in that house, and all the dark events that took place…there.

―――

I am ten years old now, and I am in the sixth grade. I share a huge bedroom upstairs with my stepbrother, Michael. It has two pleasant, comfortable twin beds that are placed about ten feet apart from each other. I like the setup at this house much better than the small room with bunkbeds we had at Myra Road.

This is my own space, and I feel safe here. Sleep is, for now at least, my one sanctuary from the insanity and chaos that is my life. I also have a small section of my own in the walk-through closet. The closet connects through to Lisa and Monique's room. There is a small shelf there where I keep the few well-loved books that I own—books like *Tom Swift,* and *The Hardy Boys,* traditional boys' books, pretty much. I like boys' fiction, and they are mine. I am, after all, just a boy. My clothing is hung up in there as well. The disparity of the quality between my clothes and Michael's is starting to show by now; my clothing is worn out, yet at this point it is still functional, and mostly the correct size. Michael's clothing is all quite posh, brand new, and of the latest styles of the day. I have to make do with tattered sneakers, but his shoes are always new, clean, and up to date. I am starting to become aware that something is off kilter in my house, but it has always been this way, and I rationalize that it is just a fact of life that I must accept. I have already learned to not rock the boat, that making waves in Lucille's house is a bad thing—a very, very, very bad thing. The price is always too high and paid in blood, sweat, and tears. One more tap of the invisible chisel, the chisel that has been relentlessly breaking me down for as long as I can remember.

On this one night, however, I am very sick when I go to sleep in my bed. I think I have the flu and am feeling very poor. I wake up in the night to a warm, wet sensation beneath me, and I realize that I have had diarrhea while I was sleeping and made a mess of my bed. I jump up and look at the sheet, and I see that it has a huge, brown, wet, oval-shaped spot of diarrhea in the center of it. There is just no way I can wipe it off and hide the evidence of what I have done. I become terrified. I know how Lucille will react to this, so I lay back down on top of my own waste and pull the covers up, and I try very hard to pretend this has not happened. I pray maybe no one will notice. I am so ashamed. I am so scared. I feel so sick, and I feel helpless to stop what I know is about to happen to me.

Lucille comes into the room in the morning and wrinkles her nose at the smell. She can tell the smell is coming from my bed, and she yanks back my blanket to reveal my accident and my humiliation. She goes absolutely berserk. Glaring at me in anger, she yanks me out of the bed by the ear, nearly twisting it off, and yells that I am an animal to have messed my own bed. Humans don't do this, she exclaims, only animals defecate where they sleep, like a pig in its pen.

I am allowed to wash off with the hose, naked in the front yard, because I am covered with my own diarrhea. Lucille tells me that if I used the tub and the bathroom to clean up, I would make them smell so bad that no one would ever be able to use them again, so the hose has to suffice. After that, I then must clean up my own soiled bed, even though I am sick. No show of parental caring or concern is to be found today. I do not remember much of the rest of that day, because I was quite sick. I do know I was put to work; being sick was no excuse to skimp on my chores. Little did I know when this happened that it would kick off the single longest punishment that I would suffer from Lucille in that house. The cellar door awaited; I was about to be sentenced to my own personal purgatory.

Later that day, to my astonishment, Lucille proudly informs me that I am getting my own room. She says I must be tired of sharing a bedroom with Michael, so, I am going to be moving into the cellar so I can have my own space. I am being given some personal space? I mean, really, can I give it back? I am so afraid of the cellar.

Our cellar is a gigantic, square-shaped area. The center portion is consumed by a huge chimney that is about twenty feet to a side. The floor is unfinished concrete and always dirty. The walls are huge stones that were carefully stacked by the house's original builders to create the foundation, with old, rotting mortar that falls to dust at a touch. The only usable part of the cellar is in the areas surrounding the chimney. There are so many nooks and crannies and corners down here, and I see monsters lurking behind each one. The ceiling is made of spaced, unfinished wooden beams with the wooden floors from upstairs exposed in the gaps. There are spiderwebs everywhere, and decades of accumulated filth that rains down from the cracks as people tread on the floor above. There are heating ducts in the ceiling as well. These ducts hang in plain sight, and the path of all of them can be traced back to the huge wooden stove furnace on one side of the cellar. These ducts have become the main highway for the rats and mice that infest the area.

The contents of my new "bedroom" included my previously soiled twin mattress—sitting on the floor, pushed against the wall—one sheet, one pillow, one blanket, and an old wooden crate stood on its side to put my valuables in. What a delight.

I soon discover this new living space comes with new, twisted rules. At nighttime, the cellar door is to be locked promptly at eight. I must finish all my chores and be in bed by that time, or there will be punishment. This curfew went up to nine as I got a bit older, only so I would have more time to clean the kitchen every night. The light is turned off at the same time that the door is locked. No lights are allowed to be used in the cellar after dark, until they turn on the light at five a.m. for me to start the day, I exist in the pitch-black dark of night. There are three windows on the front section of the cellar, yet these windows do not shed light to dispel my fears during the darkest hours.

I am afraid of the dark, and this fear is gaining power over me with every moment I spend in the cellar. Lucille is perfectly aware of this fear; I even used a nightlight to go to sleep when I lived upstairs. If she wanted to punish me, click—off would go the nightlight, leaving me to cry in the dark. Fear is not rational, it is powered by your imagination, or an accumulation of past experiences that teaches you to be afraid. In this cellar I have an abundance of fears to choose from, be it the creations of my own mind or the reality of where I am, or who is there with me making me afraid.

I can still hear the sudden "click" of the light at the top of the stairs waking me, then the heavy tread of my father's shoes as he slowly descends the stairs with belt or paddle in hand, ready to dispense Lucille's daily dose of punishment. The dead look in his eyes chilled me; he would not listen to me plead that I had not done what I was being accused of. His murmurs that this is hurting him more than me still echo in my mind.

Cellar punishment was not a common occurrence. I was usually awake when my father got home from work. But on rare occasions, he would run late and wake me to dispense Lucille's twisted justice. She would badger him until the deed was done. Eventually, every time that light came on, I would awaken, terrified of what might come next. The truth never mattered to Lucille; anything she saw that even smelled of rebellion was a reason for her to step in and crush it, real or not. After years of denying false accusations, being told I was lying, and then getting punished anyway, I became numb. I was a liar. I was useless. I was lazy. I was stupid. I was ugly. And most of all, I would pay for all these offenses, real or imagined, when my father got home. So, every night, I lay on my filthy mattress, head covered, hiding under my filthy blanket from the dark, fearing the dark but afraid of the light as well, the light at the top of the stairs. With that light would come another dose of pain and misery, another life lesson, another building block in the structure that was my broken life.

―――

My new room in the cellar seems to delight Michael. Easy access to me, it seems, is too hard for him to resist. I do not like what he wants to do. We have many conversations about why I am going to let him do it anyway. Obviously, he leads these dialogues and I want no part of it, or the pain that comes with it. It's the shame, the disgust of the act, and the disappointment in myself for allowing him to do it that bothers me most. I despise the very touch of him if the truth is to be told. So many promises made for allowing to have his way and then broken. His visits gel into a pattern, almost a dance we both know the steps to by heart. He asks, I say no, he promises something to me that might grant some small modicum of happiness in my life, I say no. This conversation follows the same path each time. When promises of gifts won't work, he moves on to the next step. This step is based on one fact: anything Michael tells Lucille is truth, no matter how deep the lie is, no matter how farfetched.

I have learned this, to my detriment, on many occasions through the years. In this house, I am a liar. Michael speaks only truth. He can do no wrong in Lucille's eyes. It begins simply enough: "If you don't let me do what I want, I will eat a cookie after mom counts them, then tell her I saw you steal one," or some variant of that, touching something I am not allowed to touch, taking a drink from the hose when I have not asked permission. All he must do is tell her it happened, and I am guilty. There is no debate. So, I get a choice—a choice on a level that is almost inhumane. I must decide to let my brother assault me, or have him run to Lucille and face the sadistic consequences of his lies. To be beaten or to be sexually assaulted is not a choice any child should ever have to make. Ultimately, after a few times that I refused him and he made my life a living hell with Lucille, I made my choice.

I was afraid of Michael, very much so. But that paled compared to the mortal terror I felt of Lucille. I was certain that one day she would kill me or have my father kill me, and into the wood-burning furnace I would go. "No more David, gosh, he ran away, and we have no idea where he is. Good riddance to him. He was such a rotten little boy." I believed this with every fiber of my being, that one day, eventually, I would become a picture on a milk carton in the upstairs refrigerator.

I do not hate any animals; I love them all. But in that cellar I learned to fear rats. You could hear their claws scritch-scratching on the metal of the heating ducts above you, or scrabbling across the floor. Scratching sounds, the constant creaking of an old house, and things that go bump in the night are less than conducive to calm when you are afraid of the dark. The rats made a haunting sound all night long.

I had the joy of being woken up by God-knows-what while sleeping in my filthy bed, including, once, of having a rat fall off the ducts and onto my head, getting tangled in my hair. I learned to sleep cocooned, enveloped in my flimsy blanket, wrapped up like a mummy to hide from the monsters of my mind's creation—and the rats. The sound of a rat trap slamming shut was music to my ears. One less rat creeping through my darkest night, one less set of claws scampering through my nightmares. I spent every night praying in my bed, willing myself to sleep, trying to ignore the sounds of the darkened cellar around me. I would have my eyes scrunched shut, afraid to breathe because the monsters might hear me.

    I am so afraid; I am paralyzed with fear. I am convinced that if I move, if I make the slightest sound, the phantoms will attack me. I can hear my heart beating, pounding as loud as a funeral drum, and I wonder how the monsters can't hear it too. Monsters are not real, my mind knows this, but that does not stop my imagination from creating them for me. In my world, in my cellar, in the dark, the monsters are real. Falling asleep is the only cure I know for my waking fears. When I am sleeping, I cannot hear the monsters anymore. I become dead to the terrors of the waking world. However, when I sleep, I dream, and my dreams can be far, far worse than being awake. I dream of death and dying, of my own death, over and over again.

    The light switch clicks on at the top of the stairs, and the cellar door creaks slowly open, the sound echoing through the cellar. I hear the heavy tread of my father's feet as he oh-so-slowly comes down the stairs. As he comes into view, I see he has his shotgun in his hands. He looks at me with cold, dead eyes. He slowly raises the shotgun up to the level of my chest. He tells me that this, this, is going to hurt him more than it hurts me. He cocks the shotgun, chambering a round, yet every time just as he pulls the trigger, I wake up, gasping, unable to breathe. I am awake in the cellar with my monsters again. Over and over this happens, always a horrible death, always dying, guns, knives, punching and beaten to death every night in my dreams. My best nights spent in that cellar were the ones where I was so tired from working on the property that sleep found me as soon as I lay down, and I slept the sleep of the dead until the light came on when the sun was up, and I would be called upstairs to live a while outside of the cellar in a different level of hell for another day.

―――

— 16 —

COMFORTABLY NUMB

Like most men I know, I have that one pair of ratty, torn-up, old shoes. You know the ones I am talking about, those shoes are all ripped up, stained, and look like they should go directly to the dump. These are shoes that you have broken in over time, shoes that any self-respecting hobo would turn their nose up at. These shoes are so broken in, and so darned comfortable. I would be willing to fight with the devil himself to keep these shoes out of the garbage. When I first got them, they did not fit perfectly. They pinched my toes a bit and chaffed my heels. But now they are like a second skin to me. The leather is broken in, and calluses have developed on my feet over time. Who cares if they make a flapping noise as I walk in them? They are so damn comfortable! I have grown used to them. They are now part of me.

Over the years, my feet have worn off parts of the shoes. Likewise, the shoes have worn off parts of my feet. Years of calluses and wear have combined to make the perfect, luxurious fit. I look at my favorite pair of beat-up shoes and see a sort of life lesson. You can adapt to anything that is painful over time, with enough repetition, with enough grinding away at your resistance. Anything, no matter how twisted or cruel, can become your new normal. You learn to put on your rose-colored glasses, your blinders, and accept it. It is what it is. Nothing you do will stop it or change it for the better, so you learn to accept it. Eventually, the abuse no longer seems odd or wrong anymore.

As a child in an abusive household, I learned very quickly that there is no fighting back. There is only acceptance of pain. With acceptance comes a certain level of monotony, of learning to suffer in silence. Punishment after countless punishment wears down all of your preconceptions of how life should be. You learn to live inside what is your current reality. It is astonishing what you can get used to. You can learn to live with any level of depravity over time. Pain, in all its variants, can seem less painful with time and repetition. You simply become numb to it all. Acts of cruelty can start to seem less cruel over time. I built a tolerance for it, my own emotional Novocain, injected as needed. After all, I really didn't have any choice, did I? Adapt or die. This mantra was a very real thing for me in that house. Every day, wondering if it would be my last day, it wore me down. So, I bent a bit more, let an edge wear off here, developed an emotional callous there... until it became comfortable.

Neglect, the act of being denied any quality of life in your own home, can be quite impactful. Yet, at some point in time, it started to feel normal to me as well. Eventually I realized I was being given just enough of anything to survive: minimal food, unclean rags for clothing, and a spot in the cellar to sleep in. Lucille did the very minimum to keep her tools alive, and I was one of her tools. That is all I ever was to her. So, I wore my childhood like an old pair of comfortable shoes. The abuse had become, sadly, comfortable. As ugly as the abuse may be, it had worn me down over time, making me the ragged, accepting victim. I had been broken in.

I close my eyes, ignoring the pain of the punishment. It will pass, it always does. So many lessons in pain have been learned. Hidden bruises will fade over time. They never strike me where marks can be seen. I know, deep inside, that pain is fleeting, so I let the pain pass over me. Pain is fleeting, it is temporary, it can and must be endured. I learned to accept and ignore the stench that radiates off me; it is a part of who I am, and I cannot change it.

What I remember the most are the hunger pains. There were so many forms of abuse, but to me, hunger was the worst of all. I tried to ignore my hunger, to distract it. I would put pebbles in my mouth to force myself to salivate. It was something to drink, to deceive my stomach it was filling up again. But the clarion calls of my stomach's growls never seemed to fade away. Eventually, you can become acclimatized to being hungry and thirsty. It never goes away, but you can learn to cope with it.

Sadly, I even got used to the bitter taste of duct tape. Three wraps of duct tape surrounding my head and mouth became just another extension of me. It became a kind of strange companion of my childhood. I could not change the fact that Lucille liked to use duct tape to abuse me, so I accepted it as a fact of life. There was no real choice in the matter for me. I was just a child. Those three wraps of duct tape around my head and mouth become a badge of honor. It was a sign that I had, over time, learned to cope with anything my abuser could throw at me.

After so many years of abuse, it becomes all you know. You have known nothing else. You have become awkwardly comfortable with the cruel monotony of the abuse. Every day of this abusive life seems to fit you more and more. You have been broken in. The rough edges that form who you are as a person have been smoothed down, broken off. You have become the perfect, willing victim. You have accepted what is happening to you as a normal part of your life. You feel subhuman.

You know, through your personal life experience and by what you have been told, that you are less than human. I became Lucille's compliant victim. I was nothing but a fly trapped in her deranged web of abuse. I knew I could not escape. I was powerless. But I became comfortable with it all, somehow.

It was fear, a perpetual state of fear that kept me in check. I was so conditioned that even the thought of complaining about my lot in life wasn't a possibility. I am having trouble finding the words to explain how afraid I always was. In the early years of the abuse, I tried so hard to be better. I thought I was broken. I must have been broken; I could do nothing right. So, I went from punishment to punishment, always trying harder to be better, less broken. What I did not know till much later is that I was being broken in. I was being worn down into an emotional pauper. What I remember most from the early years was being sad and angry all the time. With time came the realization that this all was not normal, that it was so wrong. But by that point I had been broken in, conditioned to never tell, trained to never so much as insinuate what was really happening in that house. Eventually, I was living in a constant state of anger, fear, and compliance—but sadly, that was normal to me.

— 17 —

BRICKS AND CROSSES

Wooden crosses
All lined up in a row.
Oh, so many wooden crosses,
So dark, the memories of the glow.
Uncounted burning crosses,
So many years ago.

Burning crosses.
I burned them, that's the catch.
So many burning crosses,
It was me; I struck the match.
To all those wooden crosses,
So many years ago.

Embers of those crosses,
Left scars upon my heart,
Memories of burning crosses,
Did I play an evil part?
In burning all those crosses,
All those years ago?

For most of my childhood years I lived in hell. My own personal hell, a hell that was, though not of my own making, very real to me. This hell was an imposed hell that I had done nothing to deserve. Every day was an endless litany of despair. Just one more page in the book of my joyless existence. Day by day, the feeling of damnation was always there—if not always in the forefront, it lurked patiently in the wings. My hell was always waiting to steal any joy in my life. I found this to be unjust. I was not deserving of such a fate. I had eyes to see what was wrong with my world. I just had no way to change it. But I saw what Lisa and I were being put through, and the wrongness of it. So very, very wrong. We were not deserving of any of what was being done to us, ever. But we were just kids in a horrible place. We had no power to do anything about it, children never do. I did not deserve to be in hell. I never did anything to justify it, ever. I never did anything worthy of damnation.

Well…maybe with the exception of the crosses.

I can still vividly recall the day we got those crosses. Father took us for a ride in his old, beat up, orange Ford van. Our destination? An old, red-brick church that had recently been demolished. At father's direction, we started to gather all the old, unbroken bricks we could find, carefully stacking them in the back of the van. These old, handmade, red bricks were a jackpot of a sort for my father. He was getting them because they were quite old, and Lucille liked to use older materials in her home restoration plans. This approach allowed her to maintain Kitt's Tavern as historically accurate as possible.

While we were gathering the bricks, my father saw that there were also dozens of small wooden crosses. These crosses were scattered among the ruins of the demolition site as well, laying there like fallen soldiers. After a few minutes of deliberation, father had me gather up as many of them as I could find and put them in the van. I did not give much thought about the crosses while I gathered them, to be honest. They were pretty, and they were crosses. Sacred things. I thought I was rescuing them. But I was hot, and it was dirty work, so I just kept piling bricks and crosses into the van until it was full. Once the van was loaded up, we drove home with our salvaged treasure. Eventually, it was time to unload the van. The bricks got neatly stacked in the yard, waiting to be restored by chipping off all the old mortar. He had me put the crosses in the woodshed, the old shed that we used to hold scrap wood for kindling for our fireplaces and our wood burning furnace.

I have to admit, I was perplexed and scared about where father had me put the crosses. The woodshed? We burned what we put in the woodshed. I had assumed that the crosses would be stored as inventory at Lucille's next huge yard sale. We had a yard sale every year and it was a major event in our household. My assumption was they would be sold and find new homes in which people would find value in them. I was wrong. Father had other plans. Those crosses, sacred items in my eyes, were to be broken apart and be used as kindling for our fires. How would God punish me for the burning of His crosses? I was presented with the first true existential crisis in my life. Father said I had to do it, burn the crosses for our fires. But if I was the one who physically placed the crosses in the fire, was I the one doomed to burn in Hell for the burning of said crosses? Do I refuse to burn the crosses and face my father's punishment, or burn them and possibly face another, more eternal punishment? I lived in the now, so I chose not to face my father's wrath and did as I was told.

All those damned crosses. There were so many damned crosses, and I had to burn them, one by one. I hated doing this so much. I was not raised Christian, but we did go to Christmas Mass every year at Sts. John and Paul Church with the whole family. I saw their crosses on the wall, marking the stations of the cross. I saw the giant crucifix on display above the altar and the agony of Christ on that cross, and it scared me. I heard the words of the man who spoke from the pulpit. To me, church was a sacred place, and to defile it was to draw God's wrath. Crosses were a part of church, so they were sacred as well, and I was burning them.

Without even knowing how to pray, I asked for forgiveness. Silently, I asked to be rescued from my lot in life. Yet, I kept on burning crosses, doing as I was told. My prayers remained unanswered.

I started to get so angry. I was so angry with God and the entire world. I hate to admit it, but dark thoughts started to develop, and I offered myself up to God—or the devil, depending on the day. I was angry. I was desperate. I was living in hell and burning crosses all the while. I tried to beg for help from God and tried to make deals with the devil, each to no avail. I burned those crosses for three years. Then my father would find the ones I had hidden under the pile and the cycle would start again.

I do not even know if I have an immortal soul. Because of my experiences in my youth, I cannot trust that which I cannot see or touch. Faith is always just beyond my reach, and I am jealous, in a way. I see people take comfort in their faith and wonder what it must feel like, that kind of faith. I feel I have been damned for my actions, for the burning of the crosses and for asking for help from angels and demons in my despair. These are not the acts of a good man. Yet, I go forward in my life. There is no going back to undo what I have done. But I will always remember burning all those crosses, each and every one.

— 18 —

THREE SHEETS IN THREE MINUTES

One of Lucille's cruelest acts, from among the long list of her cruel acts, involved our bodily functions. Lucille came up with some truly insane rules for the Harter children when it came to using the bathroom—or, more accurately, severely limiting our use of it. We had to ask permission to do anything in the house. Yes, this even included asking permission to use the toilet. First off, Lucille would ask us if we had to go number one or number two. Then she would ponder our answer for a moment for dramatic effect before deciding on a yes or a no. She would graciously allow us to urinate when asked, most of the time. However, she might make us schedule our bowel movement for later in the day, making us wait to go until after an acceptable portion of our chores were done. An incentive, one might say, to work harder. Go faster. Get things moving along.

This eventually culminated into the insanity that was the three-minute rule. This rule started out one day when Lucille came to an insane conclusion. She concluded we were intentionally avoiding our chore time by sitting on the toilet. If we were on the toilet "relaxing," we were trying to avoid our work for the day. After a litany of abuse about how lazy we were by sitting on the toilet to avoid our chores, we were told we were worthless. We didn't deserve the effort she put into raising us. She was just wasting her time. We heard how ungrateful we were for her care. We heard, once again, how stupid we were. She said that we had the base cunning of animals, knowing how to avoid our chores by sitting our useless lazy bodies on the toilet.

I was so terrified by her complete and total control of my life. I was so terrified of Lucille, and indirectly afraid of my father, her hand of justice. After ticking off all her perceived flaws in us, the Harter children, Lucille happily informed us she had come up with a solution to her problem. She decreed that if we had to make a bowel movement from that moment on, we had three minutes to do it in. We would have to go into the kitchen, set the oven timer to three minutes, run twenty feet to get to the base of the stairs, go up the stairs, then finally get into the bathroom. Then it was time to drop trousers, sit down, do our business, and wipe ourselves. Then we had a mad dash to run downstairs and turn off the timer before it dinged. Heaven forbid we let that timer chime. If it went off, Lucille would say that we went slow and intentionally let it ding just to give her a headache. This insanity resulted in me holding it in for as long as I could, until I felt like I was going to burst. My bowels did not understand that they had a deadline or that they had to perform for a timer, so I learned to wait until I was ready to explode. At that point, I could do what was needed and still beat the timer. I eventually learned how to deal with this, discovering the delicate balance of when or when not to ask permission to use the bathroom.

At some point in our time in that house, Lucille informed us that we were using way too much toilet paper. We were being such wasteful children, so ungrateful for what we had. She decided that we were allowed to use only three sheets of toilet paper to clean up when we made a bowel movement. Three sheets. This new rule only applied to the Harter children, of course. I think about that now, and it boggles my mind. Three sheets of single-ply, Scott tissue toilet paper. How was that supposed to work? Now, whenever we asked permission to go to the bathroom for a bowel movement, Lucille would ceremoniously tear off three sheets of paper and hand them to us. She granted them to us like she was bestowing us with a precious gift. She would then set the timer for three minutes, and we had to get everything done in time to turn off the timer before it sounded. The added complication to this was the "three sheets of toilet paper" problem. I challenge you to try this. No matter how you fold it, turn it over, look for clean spots, you still will not be able to wipe yourself clean from a healthy bowel movement. Even if you do manage to figure out a way to do it, this is not something you can rush to do. The paper will rip and make a mess of your hand. This is knowledge I should not have. What point was there to this, except to humiliate? Learning how to use three sheets of toilet paper without making a mess—this is not something a child should have to solve while under duress.

This new "three sheets per shit" decree led to even more issues for Lisa and me when it came to bodily odors. We would get our own shit stuck to our bodies, our underpants, and our clothes. We always stank to high hell of it—of our own shit, to be exact. There was no way to wipe it all off that wouldn't require bathing. So, we got to walk around with our shit in our pants and stuck to our skin. Since we were not allowed to wash, it would get worse and worse for me, till a rash would break out on my backside. I still wonder why no one ever pulled us aside and asked us any questions at school; teachers and staff had to have noticed. They had to have smelled us. Yet no one was called to the school to see what was so apparent. Sadly, curious glances were all we got from our teachers. Eventually, looks of revulsion instead of sympathy and understanding became the norm. Nothing substantial was ever done on our behalf. Life for the Harter children marched on, deeper and deeper, into our own, private, little abusive corner of hell.

At the time, I did not think of what was happening as abuse. I thought it was just the way life was. To me, it was normal because it had always been that way. What's so sad about this is, I thought I deserved to be treated this way. I believed Lucille when she said I was ungrateful, stupid, and lazy. She told me this incessantly, for years on end, until it eventually became my reality. This never-ending litany of all my faults and flaws were constantly drilled into me until I believed it.

I can still remember being potty trained by my father. I remember standing at the toilet like a big boy and peeing into the toilet, not into my diaper. I do not remember the "sitting down" portions of this process, just the accuracy lessons to not make a mess. I am fifty-five years old at the time of this writing, and I am certain of one thing: there is no possible way that I would be able to wet my pants intentionally. I am hard wired not to do it. I am mentally blocked from wetting myself. The same thing goes for what Lucille did to me. She repeatedly verbally assaulted me over and over, every single day. I was ungrateful, stupid, and lazy. I was going to become a fat slob. I would never find anyone who could possibly love me. If I found someone with poor enough taste to have sex with me, then I should knock them up and marry them. That was the only way I would get a wife. I was not grateful that she took care of us because no one else ever would. I believed all of this back then, and at times, I think I still believe it. I still salivate at the imagined ringing of Lucille's bell. I was abuse trained just as much as I was potty trained, and some conditioning cannot be worked past no matter how hard you try. If I am the sum-total of my life experiences, then all of this abuse in my past became a part of me as well. It has helped me become the person that I am today, but I am not grateful for the lessons I learned in that house. Check please…I would love to settle the balance of my bill. But I cannot return pain for pain. I abhor the intentional infliction of pain. I have, on a personal level, learned too much of its cost. I will never make another human being suffer in the way that we suffered in that house.

Life goes on at its normal pace in the house. Michael has no chores to do, of course; Lucille explains the logic of this to anyone who will listen. Her poor boy Michael is an asthmatic and could not possibly be able to work on the property. There is just too much pollen and dust out there for him to be exposed to. It seems to me that he is exposed to the same pollen and dust while he lays around in the pool area all day, but hey, what do I know. But I do know one thing: Lucille's story is a lie. I draw this conclusion from the fact that he has not had an asthma attack since he was six, plays baseball, and no longer even needs to carry an inhaler.

Monique must attend all ballet lessons. One day, she will become a famous dancer that Lucille will live vicariously through. Oddly enough, Monique has no chores, either. Lucille tells us that since Monique is studying ballet, she couldn't possibly work on the property. Yard work would make the wrong muscles develop, and she could not become the Prima Ballerina of her ballet company if that happened. And wouldn't that be so tragic?

New clothes are being purchased—an Izod sweater and Farah pants for Michael, and new Jordache jeans and an angora sweater for Monique. In addition to that, new toe shoes for Monique are a must have, and new Danskin leotards are needed, too. Lucille couldn't bear to have her looking ratty at ballet practice and rehearsals. Appointments must be kept at the hair salons, too. Lucille and the twins' hair must be ever-so-perfect, because appearances must be maintained.

The twins have friends over, of course, to swim in the pool and sit out in the sun to tan themselves. Games of shuffleboard are played with a great deal of gusto on the court and around the pool area. They lounge back on the lawn furniture, listen to the radio, and practice being the adorable social butterflies that they are being raised to be.

No attention is paid to the other two children on the property, who do not seem to fit in with this world. They all see us, but they collectively choose to think our stinking, rotting clothes and lack of personal hygiene are a matter of personal choice (maybe it's some sort of weird, anti-fashion statement). None of them find it unusual to see the glaringly obvious double standards that are right in front of them. We are not allowed in the pool; the twins are. We are dressed in filthy rags; the twins are in current, up-to-date, fashionable, expensive outfits. We are never allowed out to play, to mingle, and we are always working. The twins lead a life of luxury with no responsibilities.

— 19 —

WAIT UNTIL YOUR FATHER GETS HOME

My object oh sublime—
I will achieve in time—
To let the punishment fit the crime—
The punishment fit the crime—
And make each prisoner pent.
Unwillingly represent—
A source of innocent merriment!
Of Innocent Merriment!

———

Let the punishment fit the crime. This is a lovely and humorous sentiment from a Gilbert and Sullivan opera. But punishment was a stark reality for me in my childhood—it was swift and drastic. Most of my full-contact punishments were delivered by my father, at Lucille's bidding, of course. "Wait until your father gets home," were Lucille's favorite words. Those words were a warning, a dire predictor of pain yet to come. The waiting...I hated the waiting so much. The dread of waiting for a beating could almost seem worse than the beating itself. "Spankings," as my father called my beatings, were something I learned to live with. I endured, and it was soon over. Pain fades away, pain is easy, I learned to ignore it. Bruises heal, they always do. Yet until they heal, I must hide them away like another dirty little secret. If anyone senses something is wrong with me and dares to question the status quo, that would be trouble. Then, I would have to wait until my father gets home once again.

Before I got moved to the cellar, I would lay on my bed, staring out the window, waiting. I would wait for my father to get home to pass out that night's portion of pain. Father drove the AMC Hornet to work and back at that time. The car had very distinctive running lights that looked like a stinger when lit up. I would watch the cars coming up the road with trepidation, dreading the arrival of those lights and the punishment that would soon follow them. Eventually, the lights would appear and pull into the driveway. I would hear the car door close, and then my father would make his way into the house. Upon entering, I would hear the inevitable sound of Lucille's voice telling him all about what his son had been up to. Not that I had really done anything wrong, but in her mind, I always had. The next step of this almost nightly ritual was my father calling out for me to come to him and then getting the paddle. That paddle was the size of a cricket bat. He would proceed to work me over with it. That paddle would hit me in the back, the hips, my glutes, over and over, never leaving a visible mark when I was dressed. Of course, he always started the beatings with the cliché that "this is going to hurt me more than it hurts you." Trust me, I am very certain that it was not the truth, but it was part of the ritual. He did the legwork for Lucille's psychotic campaign, her playbook of emotional vivisections of the Harter children. Her goal?

Her goal was simple really: it was to break us down and turn us into the perfect household slaves.

Years later, upon my father's death, I sent my stepsister Monique a message offering my condolences. After a very brief correspondence, Monique told me that our father was the best man she ever knew. I was floored by those words. The best man, really? He allowed himself to be manipulated into abusing, then banishing his own biological children out of his life. Never once did he try to contact Lisa or me after we had been pruned from the family tree. He allowed this to happen to his own children, his own flesh and blood. In the end, Lucille had the only thing she wanted out of that marriage: her easy-to-manipulate husband—minus his children, of course. Lucille's perfect little family was just her, the twins, and daddy. No one was left to compete for his affections.

When I heard the news of my father's passing, it hit me hard. I did not think that would happen, but it did. My father was gone. Gone was the man who taught me how to ride a bike without training wheels on Myra Road. Gone was the man who bought me my first glove and taught me how to play catch with it. Gone was the man who taught me all the ins and outs of the game of baseball. Gone was the man who would come home tired from work during baseball season and still make time to play catch and do batting practice for at least an hour every night. Gone was the man who taught me to love the music of John Denver, *Man of La Mancha*, and *Fiddler on the Roof*. I loved my father; that's the rub. It would be so easy to hate him, and for many years, I did.

My father lost his first wife, and his fear of losing another wife was all Lucille needed to turn him against his children. That is what I choose to believe happened. Lucille was a pretty woman, and she was a manipulative woman, as well. She used sex and affection as a goad to make him act against his own blood. First, she pruned Lori from the family—Lori ran away from the abuse into a life of addiction to stop the pain. Then, she focused in on Lisa and me. Lisa moved out at sixteen. I was there until I was fifteen. My father allowed all this to happen. I am still angry at him for what he did to me, to us, but he was my dad, and despite all the pain he put us through, I still loved him.

Over the years, I have fantasized what life would be like if my birth mother had not died and if my father had not ended up marrying Lucille. Would "wait until your father gets home" have meant something different? Wait until your father gets home…so you can go have a game of catch? Wait until your father gets home…to go to the park? So many different scenarios present themselves, if I allow myself to ponder what might have been. But what might have been, sadly, will never happen. That page cannot be rewritten in my life. "Wait until your father gets home"…to me, this means to prepare for pain. It means to prepare to be lectured about being a bad boy and a liar because I won't admit to what I have been accused of, even though I did not do it. Then, an inevitable beating would ensue, one more nail in the coffin of what was my childhood…always waiting for my father to get home.

— 20 —

THE BAD HAT

"I'm so afraid...how could I have lost my hat? It was a hand-me-down, my father's old, ugly, knit watch cap. I think I might have lost it on the bus. That's the last place I think I had it. I am frantic. I ask everyone if they have seen it—the bus driver, the teachers, anyone who might know where it is. My dread continues to build up inside of me. I now have to go home without the hat and Lucille will see, and then she will decide on some twisted, painful punishment. As soon as we get home, Michael gleefully sprints up the driveway to inform Lucille that I have lost my hat, and then sits back to watch the show. Lucille's perfect little world has no room in it for me. I am trouble. I am vile. I do not even deserve to live. If I no longer existed, all she would feel is relief that I was gone, and I would no longer be a blemish on her perfect little life. Once again, my terror of Lucille is justified. She has devised a new way to make my life a living hell: 'The Hat of the Golden Blueberries,' to be forever stitched to my head for all the world to see..."

—Based on a message from Lisa Ann (Harter) Petit

Joseph had his coat of many colors. Jason had the golden fleece. Mercury had his winged sandals. My sister, Lisa, had her hat. The

Hat of the Golden Blueberries. Lucille discovered this garish hat in the same dreadful bag of hand-me-down clothing where my awful slacks and blouses came from. The bag contained all sorts of sixties and seventies disco discards. All of it was gaudy as hell, truth be told.

Lisa's hat was a horrible sight to behold. It assaulted the eyes in every way. It was made of yellow knitted yarn and had shiny golden sequins completely covering it. These were not the tiny, adorable little sequins on ice skaters' costumes or ballet costumes. No, these sequins were huge and gaudy. The sequins were about one inch around and there were hundreds of them. They were a bright, metallic, golden chrome that caught the light and sparkled whenever she moved her head. I am certain at some point in my life I may have seen an uglier hat. However, I am not sure when and where, if it did happen. I cannot remember any hat that would take the prize of world's ugliest hat away from the Hat of the Golden Blueberries. Please do not think I am exaggerating just how ugly this hat was. It was a fashion travesty of the highest order. In fact, wearing it put a target on your head, quite literally. It was an invitation for the other kids to bully you for wearing it. For this reason, and for this reason alone, Lisa's fate was sealed. Lucille decided that it would be perfect as Lisa's new winter hat to wear to school, intended to intentionally humiliate her and serve as an invitation to bullies. It would be a new hat to replace the worn-out, green army hat that Lisa had lost. As you can imagine, this hat would lead to some serious consequences for Lisa for as long as she was forced to wear it.

As we are all aware, kids at the middle school age are innocently merciless. From the moment they saw Lisa wearing this golden monstrosity at the bus stop, they started. Then, on the bus, the true bullying began. They would try to pick the golden berries off the hat and "eat" them. Then, they would rip her hat off her head to play keep away. They would toss it around and stomp on it, then apply other various tortures that seem logical in the mind of an immature child. In general, they made her life as miserable as possible every day on the bus ride to school. Lisa, like any other sensible kid, started to take off the hat as soon as we were out of sight of the house, away from Lucille's watchful eyes. Unfortunately, Lucille told Lisa she was not allowed to take the hat off at all—ever. She even had to wear it during school hours, no matter how bad the bullying got. This went on for a few days, but when the bullying got much worse, Lisa had little choice but to take it off at school again, to avoid the constant misery.

Unfortunately for Lisa, she was ratted out by Michael. He had to run to Lucille the moment he got home from school, letting Lucille know how Lisa was being disobedient and not wearing the hat all day at school, like Lucille had told her to. This did not go over well with Lucille; in fact, she was furious. The next morning before school, she sat Lisa down and sewed that godawful, ugly hat to her hair. Yes, she actually attached it to her head with a chinstrap made of cloth. Lucille sewed that hat and strap on so tight that Lisa could not take it off. Lucille did this with thread and needle, tying knots into her hair and the hat so there was no way to take it off without Lucille finding out. Lucille repeatedly stabbed Lisa with the needle in her anger and her haste, and with malicious intent, making her bleed. I remember Lucille saying it was Lisa's fault she was stabbing her because her crying was making her move. Lucille wasn't responsible, she claimed, if Lisa could not sit still. Lisa was then given a note by Lucille to give to her teachers that said she could not remove the hat. The note had some oddball yet strangely reasonable explanation why Lisa should not be permitted to take the hat off. Like all the notes she gave us, they sounded legitimate, but in reality, they were anything but.

There was another rule for this hat that addressed the sequins that smothered it. Lisa was not allowed to try to remove any of them to make it look less gaudy. Lucille kept careful count of them every day when Lisa got home. The problem with this rule were the other kids at school. They would delight in sneaking up behind her to pick a golden blueberry. For them, it was just for fun, really. Just a cruel gag and something to do for a laugh. But for Lisa, these small thefts of sequins resulted in punishments—such as her ear being twisted until she screamed, and often even more cruel, twisted sentences. These would be administered by Lucille and her favorite wooden spoon. She would beat Lisa over and over on the head with it, but never the face. Don't forget, the face was off limits.

I don't remember how long Lisa had to wear that hat. I do remember toward the end, most of the sequins had been pulled off by bullies. It looked ragged and dirty and worn out, and grew uglier by the day. To my own shame, I myself teased Lisa about that hat, too. It was just too easy, and it gave me a chance to not be the low-hanging fruit for a change. It was a chance to join in with the bullies for a few moments of my young life. I cannot justify why I teased her about it, and I regret that. I was very cruel to her about that hat. But despite my own actions, I will never forget the winter of *The Hat of the Golden Blueberries* and all the cruelty that came with it.

I know there were many other abuses, but I was not allowed to be present for much of what was done to Lisa. Nor was she allowed to be present for much of what happened to me. We lived separate lives together—thus separated, we could not conspire against Lucille. That was our lot in life: to suffer alone and in silence.

I recall one other time where things got bad for Lisa. This time, Lisa had broken one of Lucille's many rules. I have no memory of what that rule was, to be honest, and it does not seem relevant, anyway. Lucille went into a rage, screaming at Lisa that she did not know what to do with her. She then went and got a pair of scissors and attacked Lisa's hair with them. She randomly cut chunks of hair out while trying to rip other sections out in her fury. Several times, Lucille missed and cut Lisa with the scissors, blaming her for crying and trying to squirm away. If Lisa would just stop moving, she ranted, she would no longer get cut. When Lucille was finally done, when her rage was finally vented, and when the scissors stopped moving, I was stunned. Lisa's hair was destroyed. It hung off her head in a shambles. It hung long in a few places and was savagely short in others. I have no words that perfectly describe what her hair looked like, but it was a travesty. Later in the day, Lucille took the scissors and was nice enough, in her words, to neaten it up a bit, and not leave it a mess like Lisa deserved. This happened during the summertime, so no one got to see what had been done to her outside of the household. Scabs healed, and her hair grew back a bit, so when the new school year started, there was nothing much left for anyone to see.

The term that would best describe Lisa's experience in that house would be "overfed." She was overfed physical abuse. She was overfed emotional abuse. She was overfed a steady diet of malignant neglect. She was overfed and force-fed mountains of unhealthy food. She was overfed a herculean amount of verbal abuse. A steady diet of physical abuse was the norm for her—that damned wooden spoon constantly hitting her on and about the head was the drumbeat of her youth. Having her ear practically ripped off in anger for the slightest reason evolved into normal. Hair pulling and hair cutting to punish the slightest infraction was her reality. Then came the bare-bottom spankings that our father would dispense at Lucille's command. Daily, she tried to convince Lisa she was less important than other members of the family. To this day, Lisa fights her demons like I do, including the seeds Lucille planted in her mind about her own self-worth, or the lack thereof. Sleeping on a ratty old couch in the cellar, having no clean clothes, and not being allowed to bathe were all nothing but intentional neglect. Having to eat massive portions of food, being forced to eat countless snack cakes with the intention of making her fat was only part of the horror. And then there were the extreme moments, such as being forced to eat her own vomit. I can still hear the mantra: "You can't waste food like that!" This was Lisa's reality. She had to be fattened so she did not challenge Lucille and Monique as the pretty one in the house. *Lisa, you are fat. Lisa, you are lazy. Lisa, you are useless. Lisa, you are stupid.* These were the words of encouragement Lisa got to grow up with. *Kiss your mother goodnight. Tell her you love her. Now go down to your side of the cellar, so we can lock you up for the night.*

Eventually, Lisa became fed up with Lucille. The final straw was when Lucille forced Lisa to quit high school when she turned sixteen. Lisa did not want to quit; dealing with bullies every day between classes was a lot better than living in that house with Lucille. One day she was given a note to take to school. The note informed the school administration that Lisa wanted to quit school. The note also had the required parental consent for her to legally quit. Lisa did what she was told; she was too afraid not to comply with what Lucille was demanding. The constant specter of "death by parent" was a very real motivator. You complied...always. The reason Lisa was forced to quit school was pure evil in my eyes: greed. Lucille required Lisa go to work so she could pay for her room and board. Lucille just wanted more money. Lisa took a housekeeping job at the Congress Inn, a hotel about two miles from our house. Then along came her first paycheck, a paycheck which Lucille took away from her saying it was for expenses—all of it, every penny. I remember Lisa being very upset about losing her paycheck that way. Very shortly after that, Lisa was packed up. All her belongings went into one small cardboard box. Our father walked with the box to the van. Lucille then searched the vehicle to make sure Lisa was not stealing from her. Then, Lisa and my father drove away. My father came back a little while later, but Lisa did not. Without fanfare, the family was told that she had asked to move out and the request had been granted.

Lucille (being who she was) could not help herself but to interfere with Lisa's life one more time. Lucille took one parting shot. As a final gift, Lucille went to the building where Lisa was staying and had a little chat with the people who lived there. Lucille informed them that thirty dollars a week was too cheap for rent and told them they should charge forty dollars because Lisa just ate so much. Could they not see how fat she was? Lisa would eat them out of house and home. Sadly, they did raise Lisa's rent based on Lucille's little "chat." Lucille knew how heavy Lisa was, and she knew why.

Finally, Lisa had escaped from being force fed: force fed our father's valium, force fed Lucille's diet pills, force fed obscene amounts of food every day, and force fed a doctrine of physical and emotional abuse that was designed to destroy her as a person.

I did not see Lisa for another four years; I had no idea where she was or how she was doing. Lisa had left the monsters behind, but the demons spawned by the tender ministrations of her monsters had taken hold of her fears, like mine eventually did. Lisa would have to fight them in her own way. I missed my sister, but she was now gone. There was nothing I could do about that. She was too afraid that Lucille and my father would force her to come home by reporting her as a runaway if she were to "rock the boat" where I was concerned. So, I lost a second sister to our abusive household. I felt abandoned and angry. Lisa could not help me. Lori could not help me. I did not know of their inability to help even themselves at the time, and I felt betrayed, confused, and oh, so angry. How could they both leave me there to rot?

Knowing what I know now, I realize Lisa saw a chance to get out of that hellhole and took it. I do not blame her for that. I would have done the same thing in her place. The programming and fear Lucille had instilled into both of us made it impossible for Lisa to try to interfere with what was still being done to me. Sadly, for me, the band still played on, but now at a faster pace. The abuse became so much worse after Lisa left. I was the only one left to be the recipient of Lucille's deranged ministrations.

— 21 —

MY SUMMER IN THE SHITHOUSE WITH PETE ROSE ON A BED OF NAILS

I am now thirteen years of age. I am a wicked child. I am a bad seed. I am not a human being. I am not fit to live in the house with the other humans. Lucille has convinced me that I am all these things and more, that I am just an animal. I have officially been banished from the house—exiled, in fact, to the outhouse. I do not know what I have done this time to deserve this fate.

This outhouse has been used for over 200 years. Unfinished wooden floors have accumulated centuries of tracked urine and fecal matter. Welcome to your new bedroom, David! A tattered, old, Boy Scout sleeping bag covers the old, dry-rotted, splintering wooden floor that is now my bed. I have no place to rest my head, so I bundle up my disgusting, stinking, dirty clothes to use as a makeshift pillow. Good God, how they stink. It's August in Rhode Island, the hottest time of the year, where the temperature and humidity often hit the high nineties. I am not allowed to bathe. I smell of rancid urine and dried rotting shit. I have one set of clothes that I am not allowed to wash; they are ratty, women's, polyester, side-zip slacks, and a floral ladies' blouse. I labor all day around the property under constant observation and supervision, because I am an animal, after all. I am only allowed into the house for my supper and chores. But in actuality, I only get to eat if Lucille thinks I have earned it this day. I am like a dog working to get a treat, a reward for a trick well done. I am escorted into the house where the humans live to do the dishes, to stack wood for the coming winter, and to do whatever other chores Lucille has devised for me. I am not allowed to be in the house without a human being to watch me because I am an animal. I am watched so I don't do anything that might offend the almighty gods that are Lucille and Dale. If there is no one to supervise me while I am in the house, I get my obligatory three wraps of duct tape around my mouth and head so I cannot talk or steal food while I am alone.

I have one item from my time in the outhouse that I enjoy. It is a book, *Charlie Hustle*, about Pete Rose, a baseball player who I respect almost as much as I idolize Carl Yastrzemski. I read and reread this book so many times in those three months that it became my friend. This summer seems to last an eternity. As a further indignity, I am not allowed to use the bathroom in the house, so I have no choice but to use the outhouse that I sleep in to relieve myself. The smell of my own urine and shit are my constant companions. Add to that odiferous equation three months of sweaty, rotting clothes. By summer's end I had quite the unpleasant bouquet wafting around me in that old outhouse. I am a leper in my own house. I am unclean. So dirty.

The walls on the inside of the outhouse have all the nails from the shingles sticking through from the outside, making sleep a constant challenge. Those neat little rows of shingles on the outside of the outhouse mean corresponding lines of exposed nails on the inside. If I roll over at night, I sometimes unthinkingly stab myself on the points—my own bed of nails. Over those three months I eventually hand-bend down all the nails near where I sleep. I am so tired of being stabbed by them. I am also terrified that Lucille might notice what I have done with her nails. Of course, I did not have permission to move them. If Lucille figures out what I have done, she will make me bend them all back out, every single one. Then she will dole out another twisted punishment. How can it get worse than sleeping in a shithouse? But I know she can make things worse; she is gifted at that. There is a light on the ceiling of the outhouse, but I am not allowed to turn it on. I try to use it to read my book one time, but I am caught and punished with naked beatings with a wooden plank in the backyard. Lesson learned. My light was the sun and the moon, from then on.

I wonder what lesson Lucille could possibly be trying to teach me here. As I lay on the floor of the outhouse, I ponder over the logic of this. The dog, the cats, the chickens, and the pig are all treated better than I am. Why? What deep, meaningful lesson hides behind this enforced exclusion from the human world? I have no idea; I don't even know what I did wrong to get me thrown out here like this in the first place. I now smell like a cesspit; I am treated worse than an animal. In my parents' minds, I am not even human. I may not speak unless I am instructed to do so. To speak out of turn leads to punishment of some form.

My father's punishments now take place just outside the breezeway. There is a circle of stones there for a barbecue pit. I stand inside it. I am made to strip naked, for all the world to see as they drive by. Then his work begins: thud, thud, thud, thud, over and over with a paddle or his piece of lumber of choice. Incessantly, he tells me that this hurts him more than it hurts me, but he looks bored with every swing. He does not look in pain, just doing today's chore to keep Lucille happy and mollified for another day. Beatings are easy, to be honest. They always end at some point, and the pain fades away. But for Lucille, punishment was a tool, a weapon to inflict lasting psychological scars. They are fashioned to tear you down and make you a remnant, a mere ghost of your potential. Point in case: my summer in the outhouse.

When punishment is finished for the night, I am sent back into the outhouse to learn my lesson and to think about what I have done wrong. For three months, I lived like an animal in there. It was the longest and most horrible summer of my life. Then, one day, Lucile walked up to me with a big smile on her face and proudly informed me that I had finally earned the right to move back into the house and live like a human being again. She spoke to me like she was doing me a huge favor. She said I should feel proud and honored to be let back into the house and enjoy the right to sleep in the dark in the cellar again.

There was a reason I was let back into the house, and it wasn't a result of Lucille's conscience. It seems that our neighbor had told Lucille that he knew what was going on around our property. He informed Lucille and Dale that if they did not stop treating me badly, he would go to the police and file a report. He had no idea I was not allowed into the house. He only could see the tip of the iceberg when it came to the depravity that was happening to me in that house. It seems he had witnessed my naked beatings and was appalled that my parents would do something like that. I loved that cantankerous old man; I believed he was the only one who saw what was happening to me, and I was grateful that he took the time to do something about it.

— 22 —

SAME SONG, DIFFERENT VERSE

I am now fourteen years old, and I attend North Kingstown Senior High School. This school is seventeen miles from my house in West Greenwich. North Kingstown High is a campus-style school; the buildings are not connected and very far apart from each other. The distances involved can make it a bit challenging to get to your classes on time. If you add in the factor of icy sidewalks, inclement weather, and the occasional bully, it can sometimes be hard to get to class on time at all. These same issues can make it hard to get to the bus stop on time, too.

My final period of the day today was science. This class is held in the S Building (S is for science!). My classroom is on the other side of the campus from the bus stop. On a normal day, it can be quite a challenge to make it to the bus on time from this location. But sadly, it turns out that this is not a normal day for me. Mr. Saunders, my science teacher, asks me to stay for a minute after class. He has noticed something about my appearance. I hate being noticed, as nothing good ever comes of it. Observant teachers have become

Me as a freshman at North Kingstown High School

the bane of my ongoing, precarious existence. Mr. Saunders has seen that I am bleeding from my right ear and asks me how it happened. I lie very convincingly to him, as I have been programmed to do. I tell him one of my prepared, pretty little lies to explain what had caused me to bleed out of my ear. I tell him I had been distracted while playing catch, and a baseball struck me in the side of the head. It didn't hurt. An easy lie. I cannot tell him the raw unvarnished truth: "Father punched me in the ear, Mr. Saunders. Father knocked me senseless and made me bleed from the ear." That truth I can never tell anyone. There would be hell to pay if Lucille found out. I can see doubt in Mr. Saunders eyes. It is clear he doubts my explanation of how I got injured. He senses that something is very wrong, but my pretty little lies leave him powerless to act. He presses me again for a better answer, but I am made of stone. I will not waver in my reply. Since I cannot and will not tell him the truth, he cannot help me. I have become adept at misdirecting suspicion, at this point of my life. Once I am done telling my story to protect myself from further parental harm, I take off at a run to get to the bus on time. In the distance I see the bus pulling away. I have missed the bus, a major transgression in Lucille's eyes. I am now so very afraid.

I am now standing at the bus stop, breathing heavily from the run and my panic. I come to the horrifying realization that I will have to call Lucille. I go to the pay phone and place a collect call to the house. I inform Lucille that I have missed the bus. I explain to her that Mr. Saunders had me stay after class to ask about my homework. I say he wanted to know why I was not turning any homework in. I could not tell him the truth. I think to myself. "Well, Mr. Saunders I would love to do my homework. But you see, my books are taken away from me when I get home. I am not allowed to do my schoolwork in that house. Homework would take time away from my chores. Taking time away from my chores can never be allowed to happen." I inform Lucille I told my teacher that I would try harder to turn in my homework. I tell her all of this, but Lucille is not appeased. She is angry with me. Once again, I have sinned, in her eyes.

I live in a world of protective lies, a shield for my sanity, such as it is. As you will see, the lies swing both ways in my life. I lied to my teacher to alleviate his suspicions. I lied to Lucille about what I was questioned about by the teacher. There is no safe path for me to take where the truth can be allowed. Lucille cannot be allowed to think I have given any secrets away. Lucille must not be allowed to think anyone is suspicious of anything in our lives. If someone does become suspicious of my appearance or the state of my clothing, Lucille always says it is my fault they have noticed. Lucille says that I must have told someone, I must have accidentally implied something to give our family secrets away. This is always grounds for yet even more punishment. Hunger, work, verbal abuse, and physical abuse have all become the constant consequence of me telling the truth about my life. So, to protect myself, I lie to Lucille as well. I lie about why I missed the bus.

Lucille becomes quite irate and tells me that I will just have to walk back to the house then. It's three in the afternoon, and my father won't be home until after eight so he can't pick me up. Lucille then asks me why she should have to take time from her busy day to get me. Why should she have to be punished by being forced to drive seventeen miles to pick me up? Why should she suffer if I was too stupid and lazy to catch the bus? I am old enough now to be angry, but I know my anger is futile. To argue with Lucille would make things worse. To argue with Lucille is unthinkable, so the lies flow like water from my lips. I tell so many lies about my life in and out of that house that they shield me and protect me from Lucille's wrath.

I am standing at the pay phone, digesting the idea of walking back to the house. Deep in this dread contemplation, I see my stepbrother Michael walk up. It seems he has missed the bus, too. He picks up the phone and calls Lucille. He tells Lucille that he has missed the bus and he needs a ride home. He finishes by telling her where to pick him up on campus. He says thank you and then hangs up happily. I am relieved to think I am saved from the long walk. Lucille is coming to get Michael, so I must be getting a ride as well, right? Wrong. Michael laughs and tells me Lucille is coming to get just him. He smiles at me and tells me Lucille says I still have to walk. I am still to be punished for missing the bus. Michael, it seems, gets a free pass. In Lucille's mind, there can be no cancellation of any punishment she has decreed for me. Michael finds this all so amusing, and laughingly points down the road and tells me to start walking.

So, with my stepbrother's mocking laughter at my back, I start the long walk to the house. It is fall, so the weather is quite pleasant. It is not a bad day for a walk, to be honest, but seventeen miles is a bit of a hike. Almost immediately, I realize I have a serious problem. I ride the bus to school and back every day, and I have no idea how to get back to the house. I cannot stop to ask for directions because someone might ask me why I am walking so far from where I live. I am not allowed to speak to anyone or ask for help. (I know Lucille's rules all too well.) Someone might notice, someone might remember, someone might—gasp—get involved and try to help me out of my personal hell. After a few wrong turns, I finally manage to get myself onto the main road heading in the right direction. This is a ten-mile shot down Victory Highway, a long, winding country road. Once I locate this road, I know I will be able to find my way back to the house. Seventeen miles is a long walk, but I am young and fit. Step by step, I continue to walk back to Kitt's Tavern.

After I have been walking for a little while, I see Lucille drive by with Michael in the car. She slows down to look at me. I assume she must see what she is looking for, that I have been properly demoralized. I allow myself a flicker of hope, a hope that she might relent and give me a ride at that point. But I know better than that. Lucille then waves at me, beeps the horn, and drives away.

With my despair properly reignited by Lucille's latest action, I plod on. I start to worry about how long this walk is taking me. I am worried I will have to walk all night to get back to the house. I am hungry, so very hungry. Will I make it back to the house just in time to catch the bus to school with no sleep? Or, even worse: will I get to the house too late, missing the bus again, and be told I have to walk back to school? Will I be caught in an endless loop of walking? I will never get to rest. I will never get to eat again. I will die on this endless walk. I am making such little progress on this walk, yet I am afraid to ask for help. I envision my world as it will become if I break Lucille's rules. I decide to keep on walking. It is safer just to walk.

I have been walking, watching the ground in front of me, plodding away. I do not want to look ahead to see the distance I have left to travel. The reality of my long walk becomes too real if I look ahead. I notice one thing when I take a glance at the distance ahead of me: I see an AMC Hornet, Lucille's car, parked up ahead of me in the breakdown lane. I never can catch up to her car. Every time I approach it, her car pulls out and travels a bit farther down the road. I am being watched by Lucille, monitored to make sure I comply with her twisted demands. It is starting to get a bit darker out. A long, slow, fall sunset that is quite pretty, actually. This would be an enjoyable walk under normal circumstances. But again, this has not been a normal day for me. I suddenly realize that I have not seen the car for a while. Lucille must have finally tired of her game and driven home. Once it is fully dark out, I actually start to miss Lucille's car taillights in the distance. It is so dark. I hate the dark. I am terrified of the dark. I just want to get back to that house. I want to go back into the cellar. I want to curl up on my ratty mattress and hide, hide under my filthy blanket, and disappear from my reality again.

Eventually, I see my father drive up in his van. He pulls over and tells me to get in, saying, "Let's get you home." We ride home in silence. He does not try to lecture me about what happened. This silence is unusual. It is out of character for my father. I have come to expect a condescending lecture from him about the perils of upsetting Lucille. I can tell he is angry. My father, unlike Lucille, can never hide his anger. All the signs of rage are there on his face. The set of his jaw gives his anger away, just like every other time I have seen him angry. But for some reason, he does not yell at me. I do not think he is angry with me. He is too quiet. I find this very confusing. Eventually, we get home. I am once again sent to the cellar with no dinner. I finally get to hide in the dark, under the safety of my ratty blanket.

———

I was made to walk home three times from NK High. Each walk was punctuated by Lucille watching me from the car. She watched me for varying amounts of time every walk. She would do this just long enough to plant the seed in my mind that I was, in fact, being watched. I was always nervous she might pop up again when I least expected it. I was constantly made aware that Lucille might be prowling, waiting for me to break her rules. She was somewhere, lurking, just long enough to refresh the fear of being caught doing the unthinkable—like taking a ride from a good Samaritan, or speaking to an adult outside of her circle of influence. Under no circumstances was I allowed to take any help offered. If someone looked too deeply, they might see what was hidden behind the veil of lies and call the police. If this was to ever happen, I was certain I would die. The terror I felt for my father and Lucille was burned deep into my very core at this point. There was no way I would let our family's secrets out. I wanted to live.

My father always came to get me when he got home from work. This is the only time I remember that my father defied Lucille when it came to my treatment. He would not let me walk all the way home. For some unknown reason, with all of all the torture I was put through in that house over the years, it seems a walk back from school was going too far. I wonder if this was my father's version of the "not in the face" rule. Having me walk on the side of the road was too visible; too many people would see it and start to wonder what was really going on in that house. Was he afraid someone would report them for my long walks? Was he afraid the whole house of cards would come falling down? I will never know my father's reasons, but I was always grateful for the quiet rides home and the fleeting, momentary feeling of normalcy they gave me.

— 23 —

CINDERELLA STORIES

I am just fourteen years old. I cannot take this anymore. I am so weary all the time. I wake every morning bone tired. At the end of each day, I go to sleep completely exhausted and sore. There is no end in sight to this mind-numbing, destructive routine. I am so tired of the casual cruelty of it all. I look at the inequality in the house that I live in and want to simply break down and cry. I want to shout out at my family, "Unfair! I have done nothing wrong! My only offense was being born into the wrong side of this family! I am a human being, too! I am your child! All I want is everything you have denied me! I have only ever wanted to be an equal member in this family!" Yet those words never cross my lips, and they never will. Speaking up or speaking out against the status quo is a certain way to make things worse for me. I don't stir the family pot; I have no wish to partake from that bitter stew again. No one sees me. No one really sees me. They do not see what is being done to me in that horrible place. Despite my wretched appearance and the smell that wafts off me, they are blind to the facts. No one sees me—the abused, dirty, fetid-smelling child—for what I am. Because of this reason and oh-so-many other reasons, I decide to make my escape.

I devise a plan. It is not a particularly good plan. It is not a very well-thought-out plan, in fact. But it is my plan, nonetheless. I decide I am going to run away to my sister Lori's house. In my heart, I know Lori will take me in. I am certain she will help me; she is my sister, after all. Mind you, my plan is lacking in a few important details. I have no idea how to get to Lori's house at all. I do not have a phone number to call her and let her know I am coming. I did not think that far ahead. I just know I need to get out of that cellar. I want to be out of that house. I want out of that yard and the gardens. I want out of my horrible life with that family. My plan is to ride my bicycle on the highway to my sister's house. I know I need to make my escape under the cover of darkness. Lucille might see me trying to run away during the day. Heaven forbid she happens to look out of her bedroom window at just the wrong moment. So, I plan to escape on the next rainy night. I want to make sure I am not detected because of the light of the moon. I am confident that this plan will work. I will make it to Lori's house and safety, finally away from my constant suffering.

So, the fateful night arrives. It is overcast and raining lightly. Perfect! The clouds obscure the moonlight, just like I hoped they would. I lay in my bed, waiting for everyone else to go to bed. I am so tired, but so excited. Tonight is the night it happens! I am running away. To hell with Lucille and my father. Good riddance to all the sadistic cruelty that comes with the pair of them. I know I can't leave too early in the night. I might be heard if I try to leave too soon. I might get caught as I try to get my bike out of the shed, or I could get caught as I am making my way off the property. Above all, I must not get caught. I lay in that filthy bed for hours, fighting the entire time to stay awake. I listen for the sound of footsteps on the stairs; those footsteps mean my abusers have gone to bed. Finally, after what seems like an eternity, the house is quiet. No one is moving around anymore. I decide to make my escape! I get up and get dressed into my rancid clothes for what I hope is the last time. I realize I might need something to eat on the way to Lori's. I know it will be a long ride to get to her house. With my naïve teenaged logic, I take a family-sized tin of Swiss Miss hot chocolate mix with mini marshmallows for sustenance. I quickly put it in my pillowcase; the food part of my plan is now covered. With just the clothes on my back, and a pillowcase with food, I unlock the cellar door and slip out of the house for what I hope is the last time, ever. I grab my trusty ten-speed out of the shed, tie my pillowcase to my handlebars, and I sneak away from the property.

I cross the road and walk up the embankment to interstate Route 95. The feeling I get as I start to pedal that bike down the breakdown lane of the four-lane highway is pure joy. But it is pure joy mixed with terror. Freedom! The feeling of freedom flows through me in a joyous wave. But then I am hit with a wave of terror. Terror flows through me now, terror that I will be caught and made to pay in pain for what I am doing, I am running away, after all. Adrenaline courses through my veins as I pedal, hell bent, down the road. The feel of the wind on my face is incredible; even the feel of the rain is exhilarating, to me. I travel this way for what seems to be quite a distance. I see a rest stop up ahead. I decide to pull in to rest for a while and bask in my newfound freedom.

As I pull into the rest stop, a state trooper's police cruiser pulls up behind me. The officer flashes his lights to get my attention. I panic and try to ride off the road into the grassy area to hide, but it seems they have already seen me. They have been tracking me down; someone must have reported a kid on a bike riding down the highway in the middle of the night. The trooper gets out of the police cruiser. He approaches me with a flashlight shining in my eyes. The trooper asks me what I am doing, riding my bike on the highway at one in the morning. Terrified, I stammer an incoherent reply to him. I don't recall what I said at that point. I was scared out of my wits;

I was horribly afraid of authority figures of any kind. The trooper tells me that it is actually illegal to ride a pedal bike on the highway. The trooper then puts my bike into the trunk of the police cruiser. It is clear to me that my planned escape is now at an end. After a few more questions, I am sitting in the back seat of the cruiser, and off to the state trooper barracks we go. I am shaking and crying, I am devastated that I have failed in my attempt to get away. I am already dreading the repercussions that I will have to face when I get home.

I am here to tell you folks; the Rhode Island State Police barracks are frightening when you are fourteen. They are even more so when you have been caught red-handed, trying to run away from home. I am led into an interview room and told to sit down. At first, I am left there alone. I am scared stiff and shaking like a leaf on a tree. My tears have dried up by this time. I am becoming an emotional wasteland, dreading what is to come. My rancid-smelling clothes have been soaked by the rain. The entire room is permeated by their smell. The trooper comes back into the room to get my home phone number. He wants to call my parents to let them know I am safe. I don't feel very safe right now. Even in the police barracks, I know I am not safe from Lucille. At first, I refuse to give him my phone number. I do not want to. I know that with this one simple phone call, there will be hell to pay. I do not want to face the music this time; the song will be too cruel. Eventually, I give in and tell him the number. The trooper leaves the room for a while. He then comes back with another trooper accompanying him. They both sit down at the table across from me and start to ask questions.

I do not want to tell the troopers anything at first, but they keep saying they are there to help me. I can trust them, they say—they just want to help. That's what the police do for people: they help them. Eventually, I start to believe them. I think that maybe they can help me after all, but only if I tell them everything, tell them of the horror that is my life. I sense another path to freedom: if I just speak the truth to these troopers. I allow myself to enjoy hope again. So, I swallow down my fear, and I start to talk. I talked for over an hour to those two troopers. I tell them everything. I tell them in graphic detail about what was being done to me in that house. It feels so freeing just to speak about what has been happening to me. The words flow easily. I tell them all about the cellar. I tried to explain why my clothes smelled so horrible. I showed them that I was wearing rotting women's clothing. I explained how I was a slave in the house for the past decade. I explain how I worked nonstop for Lucille while my stepsiblings got to live a good life. I inform them about the lack of food because of punishments. I showed them that my rib cage stuck out prominently due to this neglect. I told them of the duct-tape-enforced days of silence. I explain how I could not eat or drink the entire time the duct-tape was on. I told them of so many injustices in that house. I told them of Lisa, of what had happened to her and how she could vouch for my story. I told them of the relentless and sadistic treatment at the hands of Lucille. I told them…everything.

I sit there waiting in anticipation. I am finally done vomiting up the details of my life in Kitt's Tavern. I am ready for justice to be served on my parents and begin my new life of freedom. The troopers eventually finish scribbling down the details to the statement I had given to them. The troopers leave the room and I have to wait there alone for what seems a long time. Then the troopers came back and said that they were going to take me to my house now. They are going to straighten this whole thing out for me. I was excited. Some sort of action was going to be taken! Change was coming! Maybe I was getting out of that dreadful place. Maybe my parents would be forced by the police to stop treating me the way they had been for so long. My bike was put back in the cruiser by the trooper. I hopped into the back seat with anticipation of the confrontation ahead—a confrontation between the police and my parents.

On the drive back to the house, the troopers question me some more. They ask me to repeat what I had told them. They ask me for even more details about parts of my story. Eventually, we pull into the driveway to my house. The trooper takes my bike out of the trunk, grabbing the pillowcase with the Swiss Miss in it as well. He brings them with us as we walk up to the front door and knock. Because the police had called, my parents are both awake already and waiting. The troopers then ask if I am their son. They say yes. Yes, I am their child. I am indeed their child, but I cause them nothing but grief. I am shocked and terrified when the trooper tells me to go into the house, saying, "Go stand by your parents. You are in enough trouble already so just stand there and be quiet. Don't make it any worse than it already is."

Then, Mr. Rhode Island State Trooper starts to speak. He tells my parents that he has heard a lot of stories in his career, but mine takes the cake. He actually laughs and says I had spun a Cinderella story to him and his partner at the barracks. They said it was a story that almost had them believing it because it was so detailed. Lucille then informed him that I was just a bad seed. I misbehaved constantly, I stole, I lied, and I was not to be trusted at all. I was such a burden, she explained. I was so lucky that she and my father did not send me to reform school. I was a dirty kid and refused to bathe even when told to. She tells them how I refused to stop wearing those ratty old women's clothes no matter how much she begged me too. All in all, Lucille handed them a story made of lies and bullshit. She is so damned, insidiously persuasive that she convinces the troopers that the lies she is serving are filet mignon instead of shit. After they chat about me for a while, the troopers tell my parents that I should get a good whipping as a punishment for telling such a crazy story like that. Before the troopers leave me there, they tell me that I need to be more respectful of my parents. My parents are good people, they say, who did not deserve a kid like me. "Don't worry, Mr. and Mrs. Harter. If you take a belt to him and he tries to complain it's child abuse again, we know what is happening here. Just don't make him stand outside in the rain, working all day in his stinky clothes." He says like it was a joke. Clearly, he has not believed a word I said. "Have a good night, folks."

Lucille watches the state troopers drive off into the distance. Once she visually confirms the police are gone, the real fun begins.

Lucille has already noticed the tin of Swiss Miss. She shouts that I have stolen food from her again. She grabs me by the ear and starts to pull on it as hard as she can. She drags me over to where the offending tin of Swiss Miss is. She is screaming at me the entire time about how ungrateful a child I am. She does not let go of my ear. I wanted to scream out in pain, but I knew I couldn't scream. I wanted to cry but I also knew that I cannot cry in front of my parents. "Big boys don't cry" was one of my parents' mantras. It was one of the golden rules, and I did not dare break it, ever, as the cost was just too high. "If you don't stop crying, I will give you a reason to cry" was not an idle threat in this house. Eventually, she calmed down and released my ear. She stepped back, looked at my father, and said, "I am going to bed. You take care of him," and walked away. When my father took over the punishment phase, I knew what was coming. I get that good whipping the troopers told him I should get. He hits me repeatedly with that huge wooden paddle until his arm gets tired. But I still would not cry. I could not sit or walk comfortably for over a week after that beating, but that was something I was used to.

I made several key mistakes that night. I rode my bike on the highway where pedal bikes are illegal. They are not only illegal, but I was a kid riding in the middle of the night alone. Lori lived in the city of Pawtucket, well away from the highway exits. There is zero chance I would have found her. I did not have a phone number or address of where I was going. I could have given the troopers Lori's number if I had it. I did not ditch the food when the troopers caught me, like I should have. I was an abused kid. I lived in a restricted world. Knowledge of the outside world was power to Lucille, and it was controlled rigidly. But the biggest mistake I made that night was trusting those state troopers. Today, I would know that those slight smirks on their faces were just a sign of disbelief. I would not have talked to them, full stop. But back then, I could not read strangers' facial expressions and sarcasm was a foreign concept to me.

— 24 —

NOT IN THE FACE

In desperation, I attempt to run away again, and I fail once again. Someday I will learn how to make well-laid plans, but not today. I have been riding my bike around, knocking on doors at two in the morning, desperately trying to find the house of someone I know from school. I need a place to hide, a safe haven from the storm that my life has become. I had no idea that knocking on doors in the middle of the night might be considered suspicious, causing people to call the police. I am once again guilty of piss-poor planning, naïvete, and poor execution. I am ultimately picked up by the West Greenwich town police in the Lake Mishnock section of town.

Terror envelops me when I see a police car pull up. I am caught again. The officer gets out of the car and tells me to stop so he can talk to me. The officer asks several questions at this point. Why are you out so late? Do your parents know you are out at this time? He then asks me for my parents' phone number. With hopes of delaying the inevitable, I intentionally give him the wrong number. I don't want him to call my parents. He has the office try to call, then discovers my deception and gets angry. Eventually, the officer coerces my phone number from me. His promises of juvenile detention if I don't give it to him seem very real. I reluctantly give him my parents' number.

Once again, I am forced to take a leap of faith with the police. I tell him the unbelievable truth about my life in that house and that cellar. I tell the officer in graphic detail how horribly my parents treat me. I explain exactly what is happening to me in that house. I tell him everything, down to the mattress in the cellar and the unwashed clothes. I tell him of the days of forced labor and the denial of food on a constant basis. I start to cry. The telling of my story to someone who will listen opens the floodgates. The officer listens to me as I ramble on, nodding in all the right places. My bike is put in the back of the car, again. Then I get in the police car, again. The officer drives me home, again. Again, I have directed the police's attention to the conditions I live in and to the way I am treated in my house. I assume that they will check up on my story this time. How could he not, after all I have told him? I feel that this police officer believes me this time. This time, it will be different. I still trust the police; I believe they are there to help victims. I have known this fact since I was a little child; the police help people in need. I allow myself to hope again, if only for just a little while.

The officer does not speak to me on the drive back to my parents' house. I find this fact oddly disturbing. I hope he might be one of those people who does not like to talk and drive. But I have other troubles on my mind to distract me. I am frightened of the confrontation to come with my parents, but I am certain that, with all the details I gave the police officer, I will be okay this time. This time, the law will be on my side. This time, there will be justice—not a reaction like the state trooper's mocking disbelief. I know with absolute certainty that this officer will ask to see the cellar. Just one look in the cellar would be all it will take to set me free. The truth would be out, and I would be able to start a new life free from abuse. With one simple glance of confirmation in that cellar, it would be over. Freedom was finally in my grasp.

I had no idea how things would play out that night. But what did happen perplexed me. In fact, it still makes me angry to this day. The police station had called ahead. I should have remembered that one simple fact. I also should have read the officer's silence for what it was: anger and disbelief. My parents were forewarned by the phone call and are waiting at the door for us to arrive. They are visibly angry with me, glaring at me with daggers in their eyes. I am familiar with that look, the look that says, "don't say anything, or it will get so much worse." Lucille starts off by thanking the police officer for bringing me home. She tells the officer her personal explanation of what is going on with me. She says I am such a bad kid that they have been thinking of filing wayward and disobedient charges against me. I have run away before, they say. She says they are at their wit's end with me. I try to speak up and point at the cellar door. The lock I told the officer about is right in clear sight. It is just fifteen feet away from us, but it might as well be on the other side of the planet. Lucille sees me about to speak and freezes me with just one look and slight tilt of her head. With one look she renders me speechless with fear. I do not want to die tonight. I let my last glimmer of hope slip away and go numb. That look promises what Lucille's years of programming have instilled in me. It promises that if I speak, one day soon, I will be reported for running away, and I will never be seen again. I will be just one more missing child in a world of missing children.

Once the officer has done his supposed due diligence, he starts to chat with my parents. The officer is laughing at Lucille's comments. He tells my parents that I had told him a crazy story, making them both sound criminally insane. He goes on to say that I should get a good whipping for running away. I should get a few extra licks for telling so many lies about such obviously caring parents. The officer walks away to his car, gets in, and drives away. He did not look at anything in the house. He did not try to check on even one aspect of my statement. He asked not one single relevant question to see if there was any truth to what I had told him. He took down no report other than stating he had picked up a runaway. Once again, Lucille had sweettalked someone into thinking that water was not wet, and that I was not abused but, in fact, treated well. I was nothing but an ungrateful, lazy, bad seed. My mind starts to fill with dread as I see the taillights of the cruiser disappear down the road. My only conceivable protectors, the police, have forsaken me…again.

Once the police officer is gone, the shit hits the proverbial fan. Wild accusations start to fly. What have I been doing, riding around Lake Mishnock? Don't I know that druggies live there? Wait—you went to see the druggies!

My father eventually gets it in his head that I went to Lake Mishnock to buy drugs. He fixates on this idea and grills me for hours about it. Where was I going to buy drugs? Who was I going to buy them from? Over and over, he asks the same two questions. Where? Who? Where? Who? Where? Who? No matter how many times I tell him I don't do drugs, he refuses to listen. I ask him how I could have bought drugs with no money. He would not give up the idea. He was like a dog with a bone. Lucille grows tired of this questioning game after a while and goes back to bed. With no instructions from his wife to punish me yet, my father lets me go to bed with no beating. We will talk about it more the next night, when he gets home from work, he says. I am grateful for this temporary reprieve.

It is now the next evening, and my father is home from work. I am sitting at the dining room table, opposite my father. I am so angry…so very, very angry. My father is sitting in the chair directly across from me. He is glaring at me like I am some kind of monster. Lucille stands behind him just a little bit so she can observe and enjoy all the action as it happens. I know I am on trial; I stand accused of being an imperfect child. Lucille is my judge and jury. I am finding it harder and harder to stay trapped within the life that I have been forced to live for so long. I know this temper I feel boiling up inside me. I have seen this same rage in my father's eyes so many times before.

Tonight's conversation is a repetition of our previous night's confrontation. Nothing has changed at all. My father feels I am using drugs. He thinks I am using the story of running away to cover for my drug use. He insists I was just lying to hide my real purpose of going to Lake Mishnock, which was to buy drugs. I do not do drugs. I hate drugs. I have watched my older sister Lori throw away all her potential and freedom by using drugs. I truly despise drugs, because I lost a sister to them. They have so much potential for self-destruction. I would never use them, ever. My father continues to make all the same accusations. I deny each new accusation vehemently. He seems to think that if he keeps asking the same question over and over, I will confess. He thinks that I will confess to a crime I did not commit. He continues this interrogation for the next two hours. It is not discussion, as only he is allowed to speak. I am only allowed to speak when asked a direct question. I must only answer in the form of a yes or no, unless I am ordered to speak more.

I am now so angry I am trembling with a rage that I cannot control. I have been pushed beyond my breaking point. After ten long years of being treated like an animal, it was finally too much to take. My limit had, at last, been reached. In that moment, I blew a fuse; I suddenly had no sense of self-preservation left. All the years of groveling to survive in that house, debasing and demeaning, myself went away. All of the care I took to be non-confrontational took a backseat. For one glorious moment, I gave no thought to the consequences of my actions. I looked up, glared at my parents, and said two words. They were two words I had always wanted to say, but never thought I would.

I simply said, "Fuck you," and by God, did it feel great to say it.

I realize moments after I say those two fateful words that it was a truly bad idea. But my well-honed survival skills had abandoned me when I lost my temper. For an oh-so-short moment of time after those fateful words slipped out of my mouth, I was enjoying a moral victory. Then, my entire world exploded with pain. When I could think again, the right side of my face was burning with pain. My ear was ringing like a bell. I realize that my oh-so-loving father has punched me in the side of my face, hitting my ear. I sit there in shock and pain. I can barely hold onto consciousness; I fight the feeling that I just want to collapse. I have never been hit this way. I have never been hit this hard before. I feel the warmth of the blood dribbling out of my ear. I reach up to try to stem the flow, but it hurts too much to touch.

Lucille goes absolutely berserk when she sees I have been hit this way. But oddly enough, she does not start screaming at me. She is screaming at my father. She is so angry with him for something he did. I do not understand why she is angry. Then I hear what she is saying to him. Suddenly, so many of the things that have been done to me in this family start to make sense. Everything clicks into place. I see the horror of it all. It is clear to me now that she has no problem with me being punched; her issue is he could have left a mark to give it all away. It all makes sense to me now; this was being done to me with intent. It was more than a subtle realization: the fact she was afraid of being caught meant she knew what they were doing was wrong.

Lucille is shouting, "Not in the face, Dale! Never in the face. People will see the marks." She then runs over to me. There was no sudden concern for my condition or my health here. She only wants to see that I have not been visibly marked or bruised. My father has punched me full on in the ear. I am not going to have a black eye, it seems. Lucille is so relieved. She continues to berate my father to never leave visible marks, for a while longer. She finishes by reminding my father of the mantra of "never in the face." Then, the real fun begins...

Today, it all ends. I will soon be dead by my father's hands. My obituary will be a black-and-white picture on a milk carton. I will not be missed. I stood up for myself for the very first time, today. It was the proudest five seconds of my life. That's how long it took for all hell to break loose—five seconds, maybe even less. I do not think I will grow any older after today. Today is the day. I sigh in relief while I shudder in anticipation. Here comes today's oversized ration of pain.

First comes the belt strap across my back, legs, and rump. I stand there naked, enduring my shellacking. Father mutters again that this will hurt him more than it hurts me. I will not cry this time, Father. I hear Lucille egging you on to make me pay for talking back. Your belt strikes me over and over. I will make no sound. I will not cry out. I will show no fear. You will not win. My father tires of the belt. The sound of leather slapping against my skin is not satisfactory enough for him. Father tells me to get the cricket-like bat so he can beat me better with it. I comply. He starts to strike me with the bat, harder and harder. Once again, he mumbles that this is hurting him more than it is hurting me. His frustration grows worse the longer I stay silent. He hauls back one more time and hits me as hard as I have ever been struck. There is a loud, cracking sound. He has broken that damned cricket bat I hate so much. Father then grabs a two-by-four and starts to beat me with that. I feel the constant impact as his piece of lumber strikes me again and again and again. Unrelenting pain has become my new companion. At some point, I have forgotten my vow not to cry out. I, in fact, scream in pain. I scream for my father to stop. I cry like I have never cried before, heart-wrenching, throat-shredding screams for him to stop, but he will not. He has gone past the point of no return. I am going to die today, I am now sure, naked, in the mud made from my tears, my piss, my blood, and the ashes on the ground. I am going to die at my father's hands. Finally, I see the end of the pain. While enshrouded in it, I am starting to fade away. This is not so bad. I expected the pain, after all, it is all I have ever known. I hear an old man shouting in the distance, and the beating mercifully stops. I lay naked and bleeding in the ashes of the firepit. Am I dead now? Why is my father yelling at Mr. Renihan? A wave of compassionate forgetfulness washes over me...

— 25 —

THE FINAL STRAW

I am recovering from the beating I took for mouthing off to my parents. My anger is growing to the point where I can hardly control it anymore. Several times, Lucille has caught me glaring at her with hatred in my eyes, and she is not pleased. When I am alone at night, when I am locked in that damned cellar to rot, I plot. I plot my escape, over and over again. Plan after plan is discarded when I find the flaws in them every time. I cannot go to the police; I have learned they will not believe or even want to believe what I have to say. This is not speculation; it is now a proven fact and I have the bruises to prove it. I cannot run away; I have learned this lesson the hard way, too. I have no one to run to. I am too cut off from the rest of the world outside of the house. I do not know anyone willing to take in a stranger. I know I need a better plan, but every path I choose presents too much risk. I am in a dark place, emotionally. I have stopped caring about self-preservation when it comes to dealing with my parents. I am ready to confront them, and I am ready to die, if that is the inevitable conclusion to all this. But despite that, I do want to live. I want out of this existence, and I no longer care what it will cost me.

For quite a while now, I have been talking to another social outcast on the bus rides to and from school. The only crime he has committed is that he is very short in a world where being small in stature puts a target on your back. We have struck up a tentative friendship—a bus-ride friendship, you could say. We speak of anything and nothing at all, depending on the day. I have never had a friend before, so it is all so new to me. He actually has parents that seem to care about him. To me, he lives in a world of privilege, and I am surprised he even cares to speak with me at all.

We are in the early days of home computers. The TRS-80 and Commodore 64 are making the biggest splashes. His parents had bought him a Commodore 64 for his birthday, and he asked me to come over to his house to see it. I am in shock—no one asks me to come over to their house, ever. I stink so bad, and I am such a social pariah. Who would want to be associated with me and attach that stigma to themselves in high school? But apparently, he does not care about any of that, and invites me in spite of it all. I tell him that I cannot go over. I have to get home and do my chores. I tell him my parents will never allow me to visit, anyway.

Two weeks have come and gone since my last brutal punishment. I have come to the sad realization that nothing will change in my family. I am now ready to rebel. I am ready to act out. I am ready to become the very thing of which I am being accused. I am ready to become that kid who breaks all the rules. I want to break the rules, because the rules are unjust. To hell with the consequences. So now, I have a new plan in mind—full speed ahead, and damn the engines. I make a fateful decision one day on a bus ride home with my friend. One tiny, rebellious act that sends unforeseen ripples through the foundation of my life as I know it. I decide to get off the bus at my new friend's house. I just want a normal afternoon. I want to feel like a human, if for just a few hours.

So, off the bus I go, with Michael warning me not to. He tells me our mother will be mad at me, but I just don't care. We walk to my new friend's home and go inside. His mother is there and comes over to say hello to me and chats with us for a few moments. She is so friendly; this is new to me. I do not know how to be a guest in a friend's house, as it has never happened before. My friend starts to show me around the house. He is a Star Trek collector; he has a collection of books and other items based on the show on a shelf in his room. Then we go into the living room, and he proudly drags his new PC out of the entertainment center. He turns it on and starts to talk animatedly about what it is and what it can do. He is fond of his new PC, that is very clear to me right away. I am uncomfortably comfortable in his home. I feel so out of place with so much normalcy, but still, I decide I like it.

All good things must end, it seems. My friend's mother comes in the room and asks when my father was planning to come pick me up. I tell her that I did not know. I admit that I had not told my parents I was coming over. She gets momentarily upset with me that I am there without permission and gets my phone number to call my parents to let them know where I am. They must be worried sick about me, she assumes. I give her no reason to think anything is wrong. This is not the place to make a stand, and I know it. She calls and gets my father on the line and tells him where I am. She gives him directions of where to come pick me up and tells him that I will be ready to go when he gets there. I gather my book bag and jacket and sit on the couch to wait for my father to show up to get me. I don't give a damn what happens next. At least I had one good afternoon.

My father shows up in his van to take me home. He thanks my friend's mother for calling and he drives off with me sitting in the seat beside him. He asks me what the hell I was thinking, going off like that without permission. I just snort at his question. I shout at him that I did not ask permission because we both know I would never have gotten it. He glances at me, not used to me talking back. It is not something I ever do. Then he sighs deeply. He looks so sad in this moment; I will never forget it. He tells me that Lucille and he have decided they cannot handle me anymore. Lucille is afraid of me; I have become so big that I frighten her. It has been decided that they are going to file charges with the state. I am a wayward and disobedient child, after all. They want me placed in juvenile hall, because they can no longer handle me. I realize that, because Lucille is afraid of me now, my father is writing me off as a loss. I know it is Lucille who decided this course of action, and I also knew my father would do nothing to stop it.

The very next day, my father takes off in the van, but not before telling me he was on his way out to file the charges on me. When he gets back to the house, he shows Lucille the papers. She reads them quickly and decides I need to get cleaned up and dressed in my public viewing clothes quickly; a sheriff would be coming that evening to serve me with a summons to juvenile court. Appearances had to be maintained. Even though she was almost rid of me, everything had to look right in the eyes of strangers. I nervously wait for the sheriff to arrive. Once he shows up and serves me my summons, I will know Lucille has won.

— 26 —

THE DANGER OF HOPE

I was fifteen years old now. I was changing. I was developing into a young adult. I was also now able to perceive how profoundly wrong everything in my life was. My anger at my treatment at the hands of my parents had become intense. The injustice of it all was starting to be all I could think about. Lucille and all her gifts or perception did not detect this, thank God.

I had been sent to the counselor's office by concerned teachers. Lucille was aware that I was seeing the school counselor for my personal problems, but she thought the visits were to help with my "truant" behavior. To her, I was in counseling because I had run away so often and my behavior was awful, not because I looked like human detritus. The reality of the situation was far different than Lucille's narcissistic worldview. What was happening was, my counselor, Mr. Scott Hartblay, was doing his job and doing it well. He had started to break down my walls, walls I had built around my sanity to protect myself, brick by brick. The walls that granted a symbiotic layer of protection for Lucille and my father had started to crack.

The first time I met Scott was enlightening. He noticed the condition of my clothes. He saw how dirty I was and he could tell how badly I smelled. He looked at me sadly and sighed. He said that he now knew why my last name sounded familiar—he had counseled my older sister! Lisa had been sent to him in the same condition just three years before. Lisa never did tell him what was wrong. Like me, she was too afraid of Lucille's threats. Unfortunately, Lisa was forced to quit school before he could help her. Over the next six months, I sat down with him two times a week just to talk. *How was life treating me? How was my family treating me?* Everything was open ended and non-judgmental. So many conversations happened in those two hours every week. We spoke of many things. To quote Lewis Carroll, we spoke… "of shoes, and ships, and sealing wax, of cabbages and kings."

Scott was very persistent. He kept chipping away at my walls, one small piece at a time. He asked the same questions again, again, and yet again. How did I feel about living in that house? What was going on in that house? Why was I so scared to talk about that house and about my parents? Why was I afraid? How did I feel? No one had asked me how I felt before that, and he seemed to really want to know. I still would not give him any details of the abuse. I knew better than that. With all the abusive conditioning I had been put through, I could not and would not tell him anything bad about my family. To speak to him or to speak to anyone about any of this would just stir up the hornets' nest that was my life. Lucille's threatening words were always looming. Her promises and threats were always in the back of my mind, bounding around in my skull. One promise was this simple, but this terrifying: if I ever dared to speak to anyone about my life in that house, if I let her secrets out into the light, it would be the last thing I ever did. To me, she was promising that I would be killed if I transgressed. It was a death threat from a person who I lived in complete and total fear of, and from a person who was in complete control of my life. It was very real to me, so I did exactly as I was told. I never spoke up. I might have hated my life, but my wretched life was all I had.

Scott eventually figured out some of it without any input from me. He didn't detect the severity of what I was going through by any means, but he had rightly deduced that I was in a very bad situation. After he came to this conclusion, he tried to help me; he had my parents come into school for a family therapy session.

The session went exactly as I expected it to. I clammed up. I toed the company line, like I had trained for all those years. I told my pretty little lies to Scott. I shut him out. I became a bobblehead, nodding in all the right places while Lucille did all the talking. I had been warned by Lucille not to speak of anything about my real life in that house, so I said nothing that would change the precarious status quo in my life. My parents eventually left. Scott sighed, looked at me, and asked me why I was so terrified of my parents. Why was I so terrified when they were in the room? I could not answer him. I wanted to respond so badly. But Lucille's threats still loomed large in my mind. If I talk, I will die—that is what her warning meant to me. Maybe it was an empty threat, but to me it had a horrifying ring of truth to it. I had never seen Lucille make an empty threat. I knew she always delivered on any promised punishments. This threatening promise would be kept. In my mind, I was certain of it. So, I did what I always had done. I lied for her. I knew that after all the talking was done, one thing would be as certain as death and taxes. At the end of the day, I had to go back into that house. I would be back inside Lucille's world and would have to pay the piper a heavy price for any perceived slip-ups or slights.

Scott decided to put me in a group therapy session for children with emotional issues. I got to hear other kids talk about their problems. I also saw it help them sometimes, but I never spoke. I would say my name during the introductions at the start of every session, then I simply sat as a mute observer. I was still too afraid to speak, even in the safety of that room. I had discovered too many times that to speak out about my condition led to pain. What I did not notice at the time was the impact of what I was hearing. I realized that just by listening to the other group members, I was learning. I was starting to see what was wrong in my own life by how they described theirs. I discovered I hated my life the way it was. It was cruel and horribly unfair. These sessions only solidified my growing desire to escape from it all.

So now, here's an update for those of you keeping score. This is where I stood at that moment in time. I was being accused of being a wayward and disobedient child. (Being a horribly abused child had never come into the equation.) I had sworn at my parents, scaring my stepmother. I had a history of trying to run away. The fact that I was just trying to get away from my own personal hell didn't matter. And this was all my parents needed to file charges against me. I was still bleeding from inside my right ear from my father's punch two weeks prior. I was covered in bruises from the beating I had received after that fateful punch. I was just a scared fifteen-year-old kid. I smelled. I wore women's clothes. I had one friend. To top it all off, I was afraid of my own shadow from years of abuse.

On the morning I received the summons to go to juvenile court, the terror of it all hit me. It was just two days before I was due to appear in court, so I went to see Scott in his office. I told him with equal amounts of shock and anger what my parents were doing to me. I desperately needed to talk to someone. I had no idea what was going to happen to me or what I was supposed to do about it. I felt as if I was crawling out of my own skin. Scott was the only person I knew I could talk to safely with no repercussions. I broke down and cried when I told him, and it felt like I cried for hours. I held nothing back. I felt so hopeless and so angry. I was terrified that my life was going to get even worse once I was locked up in juvenile hall, if that was even possible. To me, Scott was a person of authority. I hoped there was some sort of intervention he could take to stop my parents from doing this terrible thing to me. He expressed his concern about the situation but told me that he could not help legally. Then he asked me for my court date and the time I was supposed to appear. After that he gave me some general words of encouragement. He spoke to me for a while just to calm me down and stop the flow of tears. I went back to my classes after that, still feeling like the sky was falling, but at least I was somewhat less stressed after talking it over with someone. It did help…a little.

Later that same day, my name was called over the school intercom, instructing me to report to Mr. Hartblay's office. My stomach dropped—I was suddenly very worried. Scott must have called my parents, I thought. I was almost certain of this fact. Why wouldn't I think that? Every time I had sought help from anyone up to this point, they betrayed me.

I reached the office and cautiously knocked on his door. At that moment, I saw it as nothing more than a potential portal to a new personal hell. Scott insisted that I come in, sit down, and make myself comfortable. As I entered the room, I noticed that he held a phone in his right hand. Without any explanation, he thrust the phone toward me. He said someone wanted to speak with me immediately. I started to prepare myself to hear Lucille's diabolic voice on the other end of the line. *"Oh, you have really done it this time David Leroy Harter! Wait until you get home and I can get my hands on you! Wait until you see the beating your father gives you for speaking up, making me look bad, and telling the truth, exactly like I told you not to! What did I tell you would happen if you spoke? Now you will have to come home and face what I promised you would face if you ever said a word to anyone about our family's private affairs. It's time for you to face the consequences, David Leroy Harter!"*

I was devastated…again. I was feeling so very betrayed and numb. I wanted to run out of the office and hide, somewhere, anywhere. But where would I go? So, instead of running I placed the phone to my ear and said hello.

In my life, I have been surprised many times. But never so much as by who was on the other end of the phone. It was my middle school principal, Mr. Finch. He told me he was aware that my parents were trying to place me in reform school. He said he was unhappy with what they were doing to me. He offered me a different option than that of reform school.

He offered me a place to live, in his own home.

He said I could live with him and his wife until this was all worked out. He was willing to take me in because he knew about my past; he remembered it from when I went to his middle school years before. He knew that I was a good kid at heart. He said he did not believe any of the lies that my parents were saying about me. Mr. Finch was offering me freedom from the house of horrors I had grown up in. He was offering me the lifeline of a lifetime. I didn't need to think about it. I grabbed for it like the brass ring on a merry-go-round. I told him yes, yes, yes! I would be very happy to go to live with him and his wife. I did not want to go to reform school.

After I accepted his offer, he told me to stay on the bus when I reached my house on my way home from school that afternoon. The bus driver would be instructed to take me to Metcalf Middle School at the end of the route and drop me off to talk to him in his office. Of course, I realized the irony that I was being asked to commit the very same act that made my parents decide to throw me away like rubbish in the first place. I let it sink in that I was not going straight back to my house. Just like when I had gone to my friend's home two days before, I was not going to get off the bus like I was supposed to. I understood that if something went wrong with this plan, there would be hell to pay. And that payment could include my own life.

I was scared out of my mind as the bus stopped at my house. I saw the looks from the twins as they got off the bus and I stayed behind. I saw that Monique had a sincere look of concern on her face, wondering what would happen to me, and that Michael shot me an angry look, a promise of doom for what I was doing.

A short while later, the bus pulled into the Metcalf Middle School parking lot. I got off that bus with a great deal of trepidation. Was I doing the right thing? I walked in that day not knowing what was to come, but hoping the dream was real this time. This was a surreal experience for me. It was such a short walk from the bus to the main office, but it felt like I was walking across a great divide, alone. I had abandoned everything behind me and couldn't go back, yet I wasn't sure if there was anything ahead for me, either. Was it possible that someone actually cared enough about me to step in and try to help? I walked up to the reception desk to let them know I was there. Eventually I was told I could go in. Mr. Hartblay, Mr. Keshigian, and Mr. Finch were already there, waiting for me. All three sat in a semicircle with big smiles on their faces. They all looked quite pleased with themselves.

I will be honest here. I do not remember much of what happened in that meeting. Things happened fast, and adrenaline was gushing through my veins. I do remember that I was asked again if I would like to go live with Mr. Finch. And once again, I said yes. My mind wandered. I did not yet believe that this was happening. I was so afraid that I was in a dream and was going to wake up to the sound of the lights clicking on in that damned cellar. Then, the adults in the room started to have a conversation about the legal issues and the logistics of the problem at hand. Apparently, this was not as simple an act as it might appear. The legal parts went right over my head—to me, it was just adult speak—but I felt inside that it was okay that I did not understand. I could tell they truly were trying to help me. I began to feel hopeful…a most dangerous feeling in my world. Was it really going to happen? Could this nightmare chapter of my childhood soon be over? In my heart, I knew that these three men wanted to rescue me from that hell hole. And I trusted them somehow.

The three adults finally finished talking, and the meeting was over. They had a plan. With smiles all around, they shook hands and told me my life was going to change for the better very soon. I just had to weather two more days in that house before my court hearing.

Then it hit me like a ton of bricks. Two more days? I had to go back into that house for two more days? At that moment, my anxieties kicked in full throttle, and I went numb and couldn't speak. Mr. Finch helped me into his car and he drove me to my parents' house. I was in an emotional state of shock for the entire ride. I am not even sure what descriptive adjective I can use to convey just how deep the fear ran through me in that moment. I was going back into that house, the cellar, and worst of all, to Lucille's motherly arms. Mr. Finch walked up to the door with me and knocked.

After a brief interrogation, Lucille reluctantly let him in the house. I'm here to tell you that if looks could kill, I would have died a thousand deaths in that moment. Mr. Finch came into the kitchen and told my parents what he was offering. He would take me in as a foster child, problem solved. They would no longer have to deal with me anymore. I could see in her eyes that there was a moment where Lucille actually thought, "hell no." She wanted me to go to reform school. She liked to see me in pain. Lucille was a lot of things, but she wasn't stupid. I am certain she knew that if they refused the offer word, would get out, it would make her look bad, and people would ask questions. So, with their hands tied by Mr. Finch's incredibly generous offer, my parents eventually relented. They would let me go into his care as a foster child after my court date. Then, Mr. Finch pleasantly said goodbye and left. I now had to figure out how to survive in that house, with them, for two more days.

The interrogation started as soon as Mr. Finch's car left the driveway. Lucille was worried and she paced back and forth across the kitchen floor. She wanted to know what I had said and who I had spoken to. I chose to take the pissed-off fifteen-year-old approach. I had a chip on my shoulder and realized that I held the high ground for the first time in my life. I would tell her nothing. Zilch. Nada. Why would I tell them anything that might undermine my new hopes and dreams? Over and over, Lucille asked me what I had done. Over and over, I stayed quiet. This was clearly not a smart approach to the problem in that house, on most days. But I could now see light at the end of the tunnel, and I no longer worried about the consequences. In frustration, I was sent down to the cellar with no dinner, of course (no real shocker, there). But Lucille's standard techniques did not bother me this time. I was still quite terrified, but I no longer cared. I knew that in two days, I was getting out of this horrible place. This simple bit of knowledge granted me a power I never knew I had. Now, I could frustrate Lucille, oh, so much, and she could do absolutely nothing about it. It felt like the eyes of the whole town were on me and our house, so she couldn't do anything drastic.

So, there I was in the cellar, in the dark. With Lucille on the stairs, backlit by the light coming from upstairs, she interrogated me. She asked in anger, over and over, what I had told them. How did they know I needed help if I wasn't supposed to speak? Why was Mr. Finch offering to take me in? Why would such a high-profile person in the community, the principal of the school, offer me a place to live? Truthfully, I didn't know the answer to many of these questions, either.

The next two days passed. I cannot remember much about them as my mind was elsewhere, wondering about my future. But I do recall that there was lots of cellar time. I know I went to school each day and then endured a steady diet of repetitive questions at the house. But looking back, it is all one big blur. My life had been placed into a forty-eight-hour holding pattern. And despite all the newfound joy, I was still waiting for the other shoe to drop. Could there be a last-minute plot by Lucille to crush my new life under her heel before it even came to fruition?

How can I best describe the relationship I developed with Mr. Finch and his wife? I suppose it is always best to start a story at the beginning. I first met Mr. Finch when I was in the third grade. He was substituting for our regular elementary school principal, who was on an extended medical leave. He was a scary man, both to me and to many of the other kids at school. He was tall, thin, had dark, wavy hair, and possessed a stare that would absolutely freeze you on the spot. Whenever he walked into a room, it would magically fall completely quiet. He had an overwhelming presence to him that was second to none.

I eventually ended up at Metcalf Middle School, where he was the regular principal. I remember how he would walk quickly down the halls. As he moved, a wall of silence would envelop him, like the world was holding its breath. No one wanted to attract his attention. No one wanted to be the one who he was looking for. We would be in the cafeteria, being loud and raucous, as kids tend to be. He would walk in and just glare, and push in his glasses just so. Within seconds, 200 students would fall silent. Then he would call out a name or names, and you would thank the powers that be that he did not call on you that day. Then, the cafeteria noise would start up again as he walked out. Mr. Finch was *not* to be meddled with.

By the fourth grade, things had started to go from bad to worse in my life. A few teachers noticed the changes in me and reported it to Mr. Finch as was required. The bullying at school had hit a fever pitch. Recess, for me, had become the art of hiding from bullies. I stank all the time. I matched my moniker, "Harter Farter." My clothes were filthy all the time. I had become a human punching bag. There came a time where Mr. Finch would pull me into his office just to get me away from it all. I didn't give a thought as to why he was doing it. I would sit on his uncomfortable couch doing crossword puzzles, grateful that I could relax for just a little while. He would ask me about my family, and I would lie. Lying was so much better than telling the truth. Mr. Finch instinctively knew something was wrong in my life and sent me to speak with the school counselor, Mr. Keshigian. I got to go to counseling, and I continued to lie. The lies, however, did not explain my clothes, my lack of hygiene, or the putrid odors that filled the room. I did not convince them well enough with my pre-programmed lies, it seems. They still wanted to know more about what was going on in my life and in my house.

Mr. Finch and the school's social worker, Mr. Keshigian, both had strong suspicions that my family situation was volatile. But despite all their best efforts, they were unable to affect any change in my life at that time because of my silence. Mr. Keshigian tried to get me to talk about it with weekly appointments in his office at the school, to no avail. They once called my parents to come in for a meeting and for family counseling, so the whole family sat together in a circle of chairs in the library. We all looked and played the part of a perfectly normal, American family. We all wore clean clothes and happy smiles. I just nodded along with everything Lucille said, like she knew I would. Nothing changed after that meeting; however, it gave Mr. Finch an impression of the person I was inside. He knew something was very wrong in that house, but since I would not open up, his hands were tied. It seems that impression of me stayed on his mind. I had no way to know, but he had never forgotten me.

— 27 —

MY DAY IN COURT

My juvenile court date arrived on January 7th, 1982, the 12th day of Christmas. We all went to Burger Chef before the court hearing. My parents arranged to meet Mr. Hartblay there to discuss the details of what would happen at my court date. I was not allowed to voice my opinions at that meeting. (I was just a child, and the adults were talking.) But what I overheard gave me hope for my future. So it came to pass that over cheap, fast-food burgers and curly fries, my fate was decided. My entire family (what was left of it, without Lori and Lisa) came along for the court hearing.

We all piled into the car like we were going out for a family fun day. We were all dressed up in our finest clothing. Everyone had to look perfect. Appearances had to be kept up that day, of all days, one last time. Lucille was in a celebratory mood; she had won at last, and she damn well knew it. She was heading to court with her personal entourage to get rid of me. She had her doting, easy-to-manipulate husband by her side, and her entitled twins in tow. They were to bear witness to her victory lap for disposing of the last unwanted Harter child from her family.

So, after having lunch at Burger Chef, we went into the courthouse. Mr. Finch and Mr. Hartblay had arrived there just ahead of us. The adults all huddled together and discussed what would become of me. They planned out what would be said to the judge, making sure that all the concerned parties would be satisfied. Soon enough, all the scheming and negotiations were complete. A workable plan for my future was agreed upon. Then we all sat down and waited for my case to be called. I have never quite felt so alone, sitting on that bench in that crowded courthouse hallway. I sat there waiting just outside the temple of broken children, hoping that my life was about to be put back into repair. That day was a blur to me—at least, the part that transpired in the courthouse. What little I remember is that my terror mingled with hope of what was to come. It was an odd feeling, and I remember feeling so numb. That's what I felt the most, just being numb. When it was over, I was put into the Finches' custody at that hearing. They were granted temporary custody of me, on the condition that they immediately applied for foster-parent status.

I realized then that I was free from that house. I was free from that damned cellar. I was free of the filth. I was free from those damned, rotting, stinking clothes. I was free from the endless lists of chores. In other words, I was finally free from Lucille's sadistic manipulations. I could barely comprehend what that meant. What does it mean to be free? I had no clue what freedom was, having never been free before. I could not fathom what was about to happen to me. I was becoming afraid again, this time of the unfamiliar future that I was now facing. I hated the unknown; the unknown had always led to pain in my past. But I was hopeful of my new future, as well. The contradiction within my emotions was exhausting.

After court, we all piled back into the car one last time. Mr. Finch followed my family back to that house. It was one final visit to Kitt's Tavern, so I could pack my sparse belongings. I gathered up my baseball glove and my baseball trophies and put them into a cardboard box. When I was done packing my baseball memorabilia, I looked around the cellar. That damned cellar had come to represent so much suffering in my life. I wanted no part of it. I walked out of that cellar with a partially filled box of memories. I left everything else I owned in that cellar, not that I had much to leave behind anyway.

As the adults were talking and arguing about what was about to happen to me as if I was not in the room, Monique called me into the pantry and snuck a ten-dollar bill into my hand. She wished me good luck. I had so much anxiety at that moment in time, and that one simple gesture meant the world to me. It is my best memory of her.

Once I was packed, it was time to leave with Mr. Finch. There were no tearful goodbyes from my mother or father. There were no hugs or kisses or shows of emotions at all. I just walked out of the house with my box of memories. Once Lucille checked the box to make sure I was not stealing anything, I was allowed to get into Mr. Finch's car. We drove away, and I never looked back.

At one point, years later, Lisa tried to reconcile with our father. She met him at a coffee shop and told him she wanted to see him and be a part of his life. He was her father, after all, and despite what happened in the past, she still loved him. Her one condition for seeing him was that she wanted nothing to do with Lucille. Our father told Lisa that he could not cheat on Lucille like that. Seeing another woman, even his own daughter, behind her back would be cheating. I still think that his reply was beyond bizarre.

I have never once been back to that house. The ties of blood and kin do not bind me to that place. After all, they never had a chance to grow. All chances of those kinds of ties forming with my father were completely severed shortly after my first court date. Lucille forced my hand, ensuring that I would never desire to return. I would never wish to reconcile with my father. Being honest, I still loved my father. If he had shown up one day with a baseball and glove, and asked me if I wanted to play a game of catch, I know I would have said yes. Playing catch with my father were some of my favorite memories as a child. But that reconciliation was never to be, and I never sought it out. I was just too angry. My father never sought to connect with me—not once. He knew where to find me if he had wanted to, but he never took the time. I will not speculate over his justifications or his choices. He took his reasons to the grave with him.

It seems odd for me to use the word "love" in this situation. What does it mean to love someone who could have intervened for me, but chose not to? To love someone who could have stopped the hellish life I was living right in front of him, but never did anything, might seem strange. It's so hard to explain that I still loved him after all the beatings he handed down at Lucille's direction. But he was my father, and I loved him. He taught me how to ride a bike. I cannot imagine the terror he must have felt, teaching another son to ride a bike on the same street my brother died on while riding his bike. He taught me baseball. Of all the things he taught me, I loved him the most for this. He has passed on now, but I still wish I could have had that one last game of catch.

On that one final drive away from that house, I sat in the back seat of the station wagon. In the front seat, Mr. Finch was driving, and in the passenger seat was another teacher from Metcalf, Mr. Albro. He came along in case my father decided to get physical with anyone. Mr. Finch brought him along to ensure my moving out went peacefully—he was a bodyguard, of sorts. We chatted about everything and nothing, and regrettably today I can only recall the nothing. I was on my way to my new life. I was too excited for words, and too frightened to speak about it yet. I do remember one question though: they asked me if I was afraid of dogs, I happily told them that I loved dogs. Then, after a moment, I recanted and said, "Well, except for German shepherds," as I had been bitten by two of them the year before. I remember them laughing awkwardly, saying, "Well, that might not be good." But I would need to meet "Shannon" when I got to the Finches' house.

Shannon met me at the door of my new home. She was a pure black, Belgian shepherd. She greeted me like I was her long-lost friend. She used happy tail wags and lots of hand licks to welcome me to my new home.

The first night I lived in the Finches' house, I ate my first piece of steak. It was incredible. I also discovered the magic that was A1 Steak Sauce. When I was done eating, I stood up and did what I had been trained to do. I politely requested permission to use the bathroom. Asking this was a habit that had been drilled into my core being. It was as normal to me as breathing. The request got me some odd looks from the Finches, and a knowing look passed between them, then a smile. I think, in that moment, they started to understand just a little of what I had been living through. They told me that I would never have to ask for permission to use the bathroom again. I could use the facilities when I wanted. I never should have ever had to ask for permission for something as simple as that to begin with.

That first night, I took a shower. They told me to take as long as I wanted to wash the final remnants of that house off me. When I got out of the shower, I felt so clean. I actually smelled good for the first time in recent memory. To add to the glory of my oh-so-long, glorious shower, I got to dry off with my very own towel! In my hands was a clean, dry towel—it wasn't a towel that had been on the floor and used by the five people who bathed before me. I even changed into brand-new, flannel pajamas that had been bought *just for me.*

I prayed for the first time ever with the Finches that night. They taught me the Lord's Prayer, a prayer that was the beginning of my own on again, off again relationship with God. Being clean, feeling safe, and being cared for was like a dream to me, that night. This was such a tranquil moment in time for me. I can never forget it. The Finches said goodnight and told me they would be right down the hall if I needed them. When they closed the door to my new room, I had a sudden realization: I had a room! A room of my own! I laid down on clean sheets for the first time in years. I pulled my nice, warm blanket up to my neck to cover me, and I could smell how clean it was. I had a brand-new nightlight in the room, too. Mr. Finch remembered me telling him about my fear of the dark when I was younger. I didn't even have to ask. He said that the nightlight would make sure I would never have to sleep in a dark room again.

I grew up falling asleep to the sounds of the breeze, nature, and crickets singing. It was relaxing and would send me off to my slumber surrounded by their comforting song. If you are used to the sound of crickets at night, trying to sleep without it can be quite disconcerting. The silence can be deafening. The world just feels off to you. Falling asleep can be difficult when something as fundamental as a cricket's song is missing. The ambient noise at the Finches' house was quite different. There was the constant sound of the ticking of clocks all through the house, but no cricket song or steady breeze. That steady ticking of their antique, wind-up clocks prevented me from sleep that first night. But as I lay there sleepless, awash in my new life, I felt so damned happy. I had been rescued. I felt completely safe for the first time in years, or maybe in my life.

When I first started my life at the Finches', I did not talk much. Talking had not been encouraged in the house in my old life. I had no idea how to hold a normal conversation with my new family. In fact, I was afraid to talk. I was afraid to say something wrong. I was afraid of being punished if I misspoke. But eventually, I did learn to smile and laugh. I learned it was okay to talk politely with other people without fearing the consequences of speaking. I learned to be a full human being again, remarkably fast. And under the constant care of Mrs. Finch, I started to live again.

Nettie was one of the sweetest women I have had the pleasure to know. Her smile and laughter lit up a room and she was determined to break me out of my shell and discover the person I was meant to be. I learned so much in that house, but learning to laugh and smile without fear of recrimination tops the list. I owe that to the one and only Mrs. Nettie Finch. I felt so broken, and she was so patient with me as we worked through that belief. I learned from her that I was not broken forever, but that I could put myself back together, one laugh and one smile at a time. I am honored to say that she became the driving force in creating the person I am today.

I first met Mrs. Finch at Metcalf Middle School. She would ride in with Mr. Finch every day to volunteer in the school office. Every day at lunchtime she would sit by the milk cooler and collect everyone's milk money, putting it into an old cigar box. She had a smile for everyone; she was always so happy and so full of life. She was always in a wheelchair, but her wheelchair did not define her—she defined it. That is all I knew of her in the early days, but I know many of the students and staff who went to Metcalf will remember her fondly.

I learned a lot more about Mr. Finch and his background after I moved in. He went from that unknowable, terse, authoritarian principal to a caring parental figure in my life. He was born in 1938 in the town of Coventry, Rhode Island. His father George Sr., was a mechanic and owned a successful Mack Truck repair shop. He did not want to follow in his father's footsteps and become a mechanic. Instead, he chose a different path and decided his calling was to become a Baptist minister. He excelled at school, earning a full college scholarship. Before he started to attend the seminary at Barrington Bible College, he met Nettie Cahoon—she worked at a Christian bookstore down the street from where he lived—and soon, love bloomed. Barrington Bible College had a rule that said you could not get married while attending, so they decided to get married before he started. They chose this way because they loved each other deeply, and it was allowed within the rules. So, at the ripe old age of seventeen, George married Nettie, who was thirty-five years of age at the time. Nettie suffered from osteogenesis imperfecta, more commonly known as brittle bone disease, and had been in a wheelchair since she was three. She was always in that chair, but I do not think George ever saw the chair when he looked at her. She was perfect, in his eyes. To support his new wife while he attended college, he drove a milk truck. He eventually graduated from the seminary with high honors and became a Baptist minister. He went to Indiana University, also on a scholarship, and earned his master's degree. He returned to Rhode Island and took a job at Metcalf Middle School as an English teacher, and several years later, became the school principal.

Little by little, I started to explain to the Finches some of what life was like at Kitt's Tavern. I told stories to them in tiny doses; small doses were less painful and easier to tell. I was so ashamed of what had happened. Much of me still believed it was all my fault, and I was only starting to understand that it might not be. I eventually did learn that none of it was my fault, but that took a lot of time to accept. I was careful to give them the easy-to-tell details, the less shameful ones. Never did I ever tell them everything that happened in that house. I will admit, talking about parts of it was freeing, but parts of it were not for public viewing. There was too much shame, too much fear, and too much worry that if I let too much out at a time that I would start to cry and I would never be able to stop. There were just too many tears waiting to fall, and I still believed that big boys don't cry. Mr. Finch started to document the details. He made a list of everything I told him about that horrid house and family. But he got the censored story. He only got to see the demons that I allowed out, not the ones I kept hidden in the darkest recesses of my mind. I was not seeing a counselor, since the adults in my life thought I was not ready for it yet. So, I let out little slices of my life at a time to help come to terms with what had been done to me. It was a slow and painful process.

I made the Finches aware I had been getting a monthly check from my biological mother's death settlement. I asked if the state was sending it to them yet. On learning of this, the Finches immediately asked the state to send the checks where they were supposed to go, to my court-appointed guardians. They also asked for the three prior months' checks to be sent to them as well, since the money was technically for my upbringing. The Harters were informed they had to turn over the three checks that they had received since I had left. When Lucille found out that she was losing the monthly settlement check, she was angry. I understand why she was angry; it was part of her mortgage payment. It had paid the mortgage on her dream home every month since I was two years old. She relied on that money for clothes and shopping trips, and it was certainly never used to take care of my birth mother's children, ever. It was Lucille's personal monthly piggy bank.

So, Lucille did the unexpected. The other shoe I had been fearing dropped. She had my father file to get custody of me, and her beloved settlement check, back. If I was placed back in the house, she would get her free labor—and her money, too. Inevitably, I went back to court with the Finches and Mr. Hartblay. It was just Lucille and my father who came to court this time. And once again, the adults all went to the side and held a conversation about what would happen to me.

After a few minutes and a few heated words about child abuse and prison time were exchanged, an agreement was reached. I was terrified I was going to be sent back to that nightmare—the person who had filed for custody was my biological father, after all. Why wouldn't the court take that seriously? We were soon called into the courtroom and Mr. Finch said his bit. Then Lucille said what she had to say. I was about to be asked what I wanted to happen with the situation when the judge looked at me and asked where my lawyer was. He said that as a minor in his court, I needed legal representation. I did not have a lawyer, so he appointed a public defender for me on the spot. I was instructed to go and consult with him before I said a word in the courtroom. The judge told us to come back into the courtroom when everything was legally set. This took several hours, but eventually we all ended up in front of the judge again. It was agreed between my lawyer and the adults present that I was not emotionally stable enough to go through a trial about the abuse. The following was decided: Mr. and Mrs. Harter gave up legal custody of me for good. I was now a ward of the state, and the Finches were my foster parents and legal guardians. The next bit is the part that still haunts me to this day: the case was sealed. No charges of abuse would be filed, because I would have had to testify. It was deemed I was not emotionally fit enough to go through a cross examination about what had happened to me in that house. My case is still sealed to this day.

I am still resentful about this, all these years later. I was robbed of a chance for any kind of justice. I was not asked what I wanted, not even by my court-appointed lawyer. I am certain the people who made this decision, though, made the right one. I do not think I could have gone through a trial and retained my sanity at that time. Forcing Dale and Lucille to surrender their parental rights was the right choice in the long run. I wish I could have been stronger. I wish I had been able to stand up in the witness box and let all the truth be out in the open, but I know I wouldn't have been ready to do it. In fact, I don't think I ever will be.

— 28 —

ON LIVING LIFE AS A SURVIVOR

A survivor, according to the Oxford Languages Dictionary is defined as:

- A person who survives, especially a person remaining alive after an event in which others have died.
- The remainder of a group of people or things.
- A person who copes well with difficulties in their life.

I frequently hear people use the word "survivor." Perhaps they survived a tornado, lived through a devastating earthquake, or survived a horrible car crash. Some of them have even gone through long-term traumas such as child abuse, cancer, being a prisoner of war, or living with an abusive partner. Survivors all have one thing in common: they are still alive. A survivor chooses to live on after the trauma—for most, the fight to maintain the will to live never ends. They wake up every morning and search for one more reason. Just one more reason not to end it all, one more reason to go on.

Fighting suicidal thoughts. Battling with constant depression. Learning to live with all the self-doubt and internal recriminations. Trying to live and appear outwardly normal while suffering from PTSD. All of this and more can become a lifelong struggle for some. I have the greatest respect for all survivors, regardless of their trauma. My sister and I are survivors, as well. We are survivors of physical and emotional abuse, survivors of rape, survivors of heinous deprivation, and survivors of enforced social isolation.

I am not a scholastically trained counselor. I do not have any legal credentials where I could, in any way give professional advice to victims. I do, however, have some very informed opinions on the subject of abuse. I am in a unique position to speak about being a survivor of abuse because I lived through it and came out the other end alive. And here I am, still learning to live with it almost forty years later. My sister, Lisa, lived through it, too, and she tells me that she still re-lives the horrors in her own dreams to this day. My sister, Lori, lived through it for a while, and sadly, it killed her in the end. The depression that she suffered as a result of her experiences in that family was too much for her to bear. It led her down the path of drug addiction and death by overdose at the age of sixty-one. Unbeknownst to the rest of the world that lived outside of that house, we were being forged into damaged goods. All three Harter children had been exposed to the psychotic ministrations of one woman. Each of us found our way of coping with the damage. Healthy methods or not, they gave us that one more reason to go on every day.

Lucille married our father, accepting the role of mother in our life. But she refused the job. She launched a thirteen-year campaign to dispose of us. The damage her treatment did to us is no longer physically visible, but it still lives deep inside of us, waiting to awaken when we least want it. Our scars and bruises faded over time. Our hair grew back, and the dirt and blood washed off. Weight was gained and weight was lost. We now wear clean, decent clothing. We do not look like survivors. You could not pick us out of a crowded room and say,

"Hey! You there! You look like a survivor." It simply does not work that way. Because we have no visible scars that say, "I lived through hell," you cannot see us for what we are. What is not seen is the damaged psyche or the internalized pain. You don't see our lack of trust. You don't see that we so often have little to no feeling of self-worth. You don't know about the nightmares, so many nightmares and flashbacks of our trauma that haunt us as we sleep. This is what many survivors deal with daily. Of course, other survivors have different issues in their lives. We are all different and deal with the trauma in different ways. I can only speak for what I have gone through and what I have personally experienced.

My point is this: surviving can be a never-ending battle. But life is worth the fight, and that is as good as any other reason to continue on.

The new personal journey that I started the day I left Kitt's Tavern is convoluted. It wasn't a straight line. For me, learning to cope and learning to seek help was the hardest part of all. The very act of asking for help had always meant weakness, to me. Admitting weakness had never been rewarded at Kitt's Tavern—in fact, it was quite the opposite. I had to re-learn how to look at everything around me in my life. All my prior, pre-programmed survival instincts were wrong. I had to wipe the slate clean and start over. My transformation from that abused child to a functional human being is still ongoing.

When I first escaped that horrible house, when I was taken in by the Finches, no one was aware how bad the abuse had been. How could they have known? I told no one anything that might rock the boat and get me sent back. And it was not like my father or Lucille were going to come forward and admit what had happened. So, while my new family knew bad things had happened, they were in the dark about how bad those things were. Out of respect for me they did not ask, and I did not tell. I did not receive immediate counseling. I did not ask for help. Lucille's conditioning was still in full effect, whether I wanted it to be or not. My mind began to forget things shortly after escaping that place. I do not remember making any conscious choice to do this; it just happened. Somehow my mind swept all the pain under the carpet, out of sight. As a survival instinct, I guess my brain thought it best for me. After a very short period, my memories became clouded. I knew bad things had happened to me. I just did not remember the most painful parts.

Because my new home was in the town of Coventry, I started to attend Coventry Senior High School. How strange that I was back in Coventry, where it all started. West Greenwich was left behind as just a fleeting memory that I had no desire to think about. Much to my surprise, I fit in with everyone right away. The ghost of Harter Farter had been left behind. I walked down the halls of my new school with clean clothes and my head up, carrying none of the baggage of my old life. The hell I had left behind just days before me was nothing but a fading memory. I discovered I could hang out with every single high school clique and fit in. All those years of learning to adapt or suffer the consequences were paying off. I had unintentionally been forged into the perfect chameleon. I could become what was needed by every group I was with. I even put on my happy face and smiled at everyone like I had been trained to. But inside, I was still so damned broken. I should have been on cloud nine, but instead I felt like an imposter walking those halls. I felt I did not belong there with the normal kids. If they knew what I had allowed to be done to me, they would have run away screaming or shunned me at best, I thought. But they never saw me for what I thought I was—a broken, perverted, dirty thing. How could they not see it?

I fit in at my new school, somehow. But I didn't know how to cope with my new reality. I had no experience with people actually liking me. Sadly, this very act of fitting in—something I had longed for, for so long—made me feel broken and alone. I felt alone because I realized it was all an act; I was living on a paint-by-the-numbers canvas. I knew where to put the colors. I just did not understand why.

I went to all my classes at my new school, just like I always had before. I loved school. School had been my escape from that damned house. I joined the Air Force Junior Reserve Officer Training Corps (AFJROTC) because I loved the concept of the military. (I had been involved in the Navy version at North Kingstown High School.) I even met a pretty girl in my homeroom class and asked her to the military ball, a formal dance. I used the stupidest pick-up line ever: "Hello, I'm lonely." After that stellar conversation opener, I asked her to the dance and, oddly enough, she said yes.

So, I now had a girlfriend. We would even walk down the halls of the high school holding hands. At every school dance and formal, we danced like we didn't care. We sat on the sofa at her parents' house on Sunday afternoons. We watched the rocket launch every hour on MTV. As I said, I fit in with everyone in my new life. I had new parents who cared for me. I had new friends in my life. I even had a girlfriend that I cared for very much. I had all of that, but on the inside, I was crying. My smile was always painted on, just an act. I was adept at just fitting in and not making waves.

Despite my new life, Lucille's programming still held firm, and every night I dreamed my way back into that house. I signed up for every after-school activity imaginable, trying to shake off my past and feel like I belonged. I just wanted to feel like I was a part of something. I went to every school dance. I danced at them like a maniac even though I had no idea how to do it. I joined the color guard. I joined the rifle drill team. I tried to do all the things the popular kids do. I did all of this and more. But none of it worked; I still felt like I was on the outside wanting to get in. Please, won't someone let me in? How can you make friends when you trust no one? How can you let people in when you can't let down your guard? How can you trust someone when you are afraid of your own shadow? I don't believe I really did fit in at that school. People will say they remember me: I was that quiet kid who got along with everyone.

My quality of life improved so much when I was taken in by the Finches, but the emotional scars and memories formed from years of abuse were still there just ticking away, waiting to explode. Those

My Senior graduation picture

monsters were always lurking, hiding, waiting for the trigger that would let them out to play. My new parents never knew the extent that I suffered; I had received no counseling about it at all because I did not tell them. I could not talk about it with them. It was too much pain and too much shame. It was just too hard to open up the terrible details of what happened to me in that house.

When I would get a memory back, it would be horrible. I once saw someone get hit in anger with a two-by-four outside a bar. *A two-by-four*...then I remembered my personal experience being beaten, and then so much more. The moments came flooding back and froze me in place. They did not come back in a slow trickle—I might have been able to cope with that, barely—but the floodgates opened all at once.

I nearly drowned in my memories that night. In my mind, I knew that all those things had happened to me. But I had dulled the edges of the memories—blunted them, so to speak. Those memories no longer cut me to the quick. But for them all to come flooding out at once was devastating. I quite literally wanted to kill myself after reliving it all. The terror had returned. I started to shake. My heart was racing. I could barely breathe. I even convinced myself that I needed to hurt myself to make the memories go away. I went home and closed myself off in my bedroom. I did not want to ever come out.

Soon I was at my computer, typing away. I started writing morbid poetry, bad poetry about death and committing suicide. I eventually broke down and spoke to Mr. Finch about how I felt. He thought the best course of action would be to pray the bad away, but I knew that I needed more than prayer this time. I had no idea what I needed; I just knew that prayer was not working. He became worried about me. He was concerned that I was sleeping so much, but I continued to stay in my room and write, only leaving for meals and absolute necessities.

Eventually Mr. Finch became so concerned about my mental health that he sent me to see a psychiatrist. I was offered the choice: go see this doctor or move out. He could not bear to see me self-destruct in this way. If I wanted to kill myself, I would have to do it somewhere else. I was depressed and unemployed, not stupid, so I went to the appointment.

On my first visit I stared at the ceiling a bit, dodged questions, and made no effort to try to speak about anything of importance. But I kept going to these appointments every week, as I really had no choice. Soon, I started to listen to what the psychiatrist was saying. He asked very pointed questions. Dangerous questions. He asked questions that no one else asked me before, and his questions tore my heart to pieces. He asked the kind of questions that forced me to face the truth about my childhood. I tried to dodge and prevaricate the best I could. I was a master of the subtle subject change, *no questions about me, please*. I was the artful dodger of any question that led to self-examination. But he would not be sidetracked, and he persisted. In the end, his persistence beat my resistance and the truth came trickling out.

My truths emerged in small doses. Small doses were all I could take. I could not reveal it all at one time. My mind would crack just a little bit more with each question I answered, and each story that I told. The counselor said it was no wonder I was depressed; I had been holding onto all that horror for so long. I was immediately put on Prozac, the new wonder pill of the day. It did not work, and my depression got much worse. I continued to hide in my bedroom, trying to sleep my life away in twelve-hour increments. And I continued to write even more morbid poetry during my waking hours.

Mr. Finch went into my room one day when I went out to grab a pack of smokes, and he read my poems. Unbeknownst to me, he called my psychiatrist and spoke to him about what I had written. They decided I needed to be hospitalized right away, willingly or not. As soon as I got home, Mr. Finch drove me over to see the psychiatrist. When I got there, printouts of my poems were placed in front of me and I was given a choice: self-commit, or they would have me involuntarily committed. Discretion being the better part of valor, I agreed that yes, I would go. I knew I was quite ill and that I needed to get some help. I knew I needed to stop thinking about killing myself. At that moment in my life, I had made the decision that I no longer wanted to continue living. So many bad things had happened to me and I was in constant turmoil, tortured by the pain of dealing with my past. I felt in my heart that I was to blame for it all. My mind knew, logically, that it was not my fault, but it was a losing the battle. So, we drove home, I packed a bag, and off to Butler Hospital we went.

I self-committed myself that night. I went into a few small rooms where people were sitting at their desks. I had conversations with a few of those people. After I was done talking, they gave me a form to sign, and I officially became a guest of Butler Hospital. The forms stated that I could check in, but I could not check out unless they said I could. I had told them the truth, dark as it was. I felt that my suicide was the only way out. There was just too much pain in my life and I did not want to go on. Funny thing…if you say this in a mental hospital, they won't let you walk out the door. I could read the writing on the wall once I told them I felt suicidal. Three gigantic orderlies came and stood at my door with arms crossed, assigned to keep their eyes on me. I was going nowhere. But as mixed-up as I was, I knew on some level that I needed to be there. Here, I was kept safe from self-harm.

I spent the next three months in the alcohol and drug treatment ward. There was no one close to my age to me on the normal psychiatric ward, so they thought it would be better for me to be with people closer to my age. I had to attend all the meetings on the floor, no exceptions. So, I went to the Alcoholic Anonymous and Narcotics Anonymous meetings every day. They were all addiction-themed groups. Not a single group I went to dealt with anything that was remotely wrong with me.

At first, I resented being forced to go to endless AA and NA meetings. I hate drugs and was not a big drinker. What did an addict or a drunk know about my pain? I found something out on that ward, however: they knew plenty about pain. I was not alone after all. All the patients on the ward were suffering. We were all broken, somehow. I soaked it all in like a sponge. I learned so much from the other broken people on that ward. I discovered that it did not matter in the end if you were a drunk, or an addict, or a victim of abuse. We all knew of loss and pain, and we all knew intimately about self-hatred. We all blamed ourselves. I recall having deeply emotional conversations with fellow patients over games of pool, and I spoke about all my nightmares to my mental health aide over games of ping pong.

The best place to talk and to really let it out was the smoking room, because the doctors and case workers never set foot into that room. It was our safe place, our sanctuary. We would sit in those chairs and talk for hours on end. I learned so much about survival in that room just by speaking with the other patients and seeing their pain. I heard so many stories of self-destruction and self-loathing. One I recall is of a man who got too drunk to go to his mother's funeral and the grief and shame he felt for that action. Another story was of someone losing their house because they spent the mortgage money on their drug of choice. People talked of how their own families shunned them and had given up on them. These people were at rock bottom and had to be somewhere they could let it all out. I started to talk of my past as well in that room. We had a nicotine fueled form of quid pro quo. We swapped our darkest memories of personal disaster while we sat there and smoked. I could not speak as openly to any doctor like the way I spoke in that room. I could not share like I shared in that room. I learned in that room that everyone feels pain in some form. I also learned that some people could deal with it better than I could. We spoke of things we could not tell our doctors, those dirty little secrets that they would not understand. To understand, they would have had to have lived it like we had. So here, we shared little pieces of our lives with each other. Tearful story by tearful story, we tried to help each other the only way we knew how. The tears would flow freely while we sat and smoked together. In that smoking room, we each felt a little less lonely, at least for a while.

I met with several psychiatrists during my stay at Butler. Several lasted about five minutes as my doctor. The first one walked into the room with my chart in his hand that had all the carefully taken notes about me from the past week written up by my case worker. The notes included all my history from that house I could remember. I assumed the doctor had read the notes before coming into the room. That's what the notes were for, or so I assumed. I was prepared for a bit of small talk just to break the ice a little, then after that, we would get down to business.

He then informed me that the first thing I needed to do was forgive my parents. According to him, I would not begin to heal until I forgave them for everything they did to me. I was floored by this declaration. I stood up, told him to F-off, then left the office, trying to slam the door behind me (the door operated by hydraulics so it was not as satisfying as I hoped it would be).

A few minutes later, my case worker found me angrily puffing away at a cigarette in the smoking room. He asked me why I had stormed out of my appointment the way I did saying the doctor wanted me to go back in and finish my session with him. The censored version of my answer is quite simple; I was never going to speak to that doctor again. Seriously? There was no way in hell I was ever going to forgive my parents. Forgiveness was never going to happen; I would never speak those words. They could not make me forgive them. I simply could not do it. I did not have that kind of mercy for them inside me. I rambled on for quite some time on that subject.

My case worker agreed with me wholeheartedly. Some people just do not deserve forgiveness, he said. He wrote a note concerning this on my chart as I watched. I am certain this was only done to mollify me. Then he left the room while I continued to smoke like a chimney.

So, here's the best part. A week later, I walk into Doctor Number Two's office for a new appointment. He introduced himself, then I sat down and settled in to wait for the healing to begin. He looked at my chart, then slowly back up at me and said, you guessed it: "You are going to have to forgive them."

I freaked out in a big way. I shouted, "Are you F---ing kidding me?" and stormed out of the room, again. I tried to slam the door behind me, again. Damn hydraulics messed up my dramatic exit, again.

Cut back to the smoking room—my case worker shakes his head in disbelief that this happened a second time. He writes the same note on the chart again, this time in bigger letters. All the while, I am puffing away on my cigarette like a dragon.

The next morning, I was brought to yet another doctor's office. She introduces herself to me and before she can say another word, I ask her right up front: "Are you going to tell me to forgive my parents?" She smiled sadly and told me that I may never be able to forgive them. But that was okay, she said. I didn't need to forgive them to start healing. I liked her immediately. I eventually learned that I held no blame in what had been done to me. These things were done *to* me, she insisted, and were not my fault. Eventually I came to believe that basic truth about my childhood, but it would take time.

I also learned that psychiatrists love to give out pills. Better living through chemistry, I guess. During my stay at Butler, they had me try so many of them, and every one of these pills came with their own individual side effects. It became a process of trial and error. They kept looking for that one perfect pill or combination of pills to help find the best results to deal with my depression. Side effects were a secondary concern for them; they felt they needed to knock the depression down first. Once the right medication was found, *then* adjustments could be made to limit side effects. I eventually ended up on lithium. I hated the side effects. My hands trembled and shook nonstop. I was nauseous all the time. I was informed that if I stuck with my regimen, the side effects would eventually level out. They insisted the side effects might even go away with time as my body adjusted. I was willing to deal with those issues on the short term, as long as it helped with the long-term issues of depression and suicidal thoughts. Once I was on lithium for a week, they deemed I was ready to go home. As I packed my bag to leave, I found that I was worried about going back out into the real world. I wasn't sure I could handle it.

I was finally discharged after three months at Butler Hospital. But there was real-life drama unfolding in the Finch household the night I got home. (Bad timing: there is a first time for everything, I suppose.) I had only been home a short time when there was a physical altercation in the house. It had nothing to do with me. The fight was between Mr. Finch and someone else. Suffice it to say, when I saw punches being thrown it set me back, emotionally. Once the fight was over and everyone had calmed down, Mr. Finch came looking for me. He found me hiding in my closet, rocking back and forth with a knife in my hand, crying. I was ready to cut myself, just trying to work up the courage. So, back to Butler Hospital I went, for another month and a half.

Back to the psych ward. More talking. A lot of ping pong. So many new medications tried in combination with the lithium.

Finally, I got out of the hospital…again. This time I felt great, much better than before I went in. I went to a few of my outpatient appointments and took my pills regularly for a month or so. I felt fine, but I hated the side effects of my medications. As a matter of fact, often I would feel right as rain and then have to go in and talk to my counselor. It would stir up all the pain and bad memories again. Sometimes it would take a week to recover. Then I would have to go back in and be stirred up all over again. At some point in this torturous process, I decided I was cured. I no longer needed counseling or any of the medications anymore.

I did not know it at the time, but this turned out to be a huge mistake. This decision started a recurring pattern in my life. I would be fine for a while, then sink into depression, seek help, get medications, feel better, and then stop treatment all over again.

Because of this, it is astonishing to me that I committed myself to Eye Movement Desensitization and Reprocessing (EMDR) for my PTSD. EMDR is a relatively new form of therapy for people afflicted with PTSD that helps the brain process old memories through eye movements. Thirty-one sessions later, I walked out with almost no remaining symptoms. I did not quit this time; I did not give up in despair like every time before. I stayed the course for once, after all the years of walking away. I would not be where I am now in my life without finishing that treatment. I am glad I broke the cycle. I am a survivor in more than name now. I survived Lucille; she can't hurt me anymore. I can now even speak of my past without falling into a depression.

I am a survivor.

— 29 —

IN THE DARKNESS, I DREAMED

I am fifteen years old. I still sleep in my own personal purgatory, that damned cellar. An old, decrepit couch is now my bed. It is a couch that has absorbed all the eye-watering, rancid miasma that pours off of my unwashed body each night. When I try to sleep, I have one constant companion: fear of the dark. I live in a perpetual state of fear. I hate this life I live. The word "anger" will no longer suffice to describe how I feel toward my parents. My life has become a never-ending cycle of destruction. Abuse at the house. Bullying at school. Constant nightmares as I sleep. Every day I have to do more and more forced labor around the property. All of this happens because the psychotic puppet-master, my stepmother, is pulling all the strings. Maybe I eat tonight, maybe I don't. Maybe I get beat tonight, maybe I don't. Maybe I will bathe tonight, but I know I won't. Maybe I will wake from this horrible dream tomorrow, yet I know I won't. My life has become a never-ending procession of worsening humiliations. Pain, broken promises, lies, disappointments, and more pain have become the normal for me. Every night, as I lay in the darkness, I would scheme. Every night, I slept trapped in the cellar. But in the darkness, at least I could dream...

No one but I knows how close I was to losing my mind at the end of my days inside Kitt's Tavern. I would not have lasted much longer in that house; I am certain of that. Rescue arrived just in time. I was ready and prepared to lash out at all the creators and dealers of the pain in my life. I had only two choices remaining in my world. The first was to lash out physically. I would seek revenge and give all of the pain back, returning the full measure of the suffering I had endured. This would allow me to take charge and regain some control of my life. The second choice was to kill myself. This would have been the ultimate act of control. In that final act, no one would ever be able to regain control of my life. My life, my choice. My very life hung in the balance of my uncertainty, the scales of my life tipping precariously to and fro, between one choice and the other. My fear of the finality of death was my only deterrent to that very final act. I could not bring myself to act on what I would fantasize about.

Every night I dream endlessly of death. Dreams of my own demise at the hands of my parents are my nightly companion. I have had nightmares of my own violent death for so many years, so many times. But as I have gotten older, I see things with more clarity. I see the world that I live in is broken; it is a violent and cruel world. Now I find myself angry all the time. With every act of violence and abuse against me, my anger grows. I have started to think the unthinkable, I have started to think about lashing out, and fighting back at the unrelenting abuse that has been my life. Fighting back has never been an option before now. I have been too well-trained to be submissive. I live in fear of my life, as I have been made to. I am too well conditioned to do such a thing. I can do them no harm. But in the darkness, I dreamed.

Dreams of violence. I remember them too well. Recollections of those dreams and what they represented still haunt me today. These were dreams that stayed in my thoughts long after I woke up in the morning, growing in my mind like a tumor. I almost lost control in the end; I am eternally grateful I did not. The very act of losing control and lashing out in violence would have damned me. If I had returned violence for violence, I would have become the very thing they said I was: a monster in a child's body, a wolf in sheep's clothing, a rotten child, a bad seed. I could not take my own life. I could not retaliate for the years of pain, but alone in the darkness, I could dream.

There is a shotgun in the house. It is my father's gun. It is kept safe in the master bedroom closet, hidden behind the door. I wonder at the logic of keeping a gun in a house where abuse is commonplace. Are they really so certain I will not lash out and use that gun on them? In my dreams I had so many plans involving that gun. And these plans included my parents. There were so many satisfying, violent plans with no thought of the consequences. In my dreams, there are never consequences. In the beginning, my dreams were of actions that could be done in real life utilizing common items that existed in the house to enact my vengeance. Had I ever been able to get over my fear of my parents, I know I would have used them. On days I did not fear them, my mind would get more creative. The ways I would destroy my antagonists became twisted. I had started to think outside of my house-shaped box. I knew I could never do any of these things...or could I?

Lucille. Everything always came back to Lucille. She was the author of my childhood—word by painful word, she wrote my existence in blood. I had become Harter Farter to the bullies of the world. I had no chance to be normal. I was not allowed to fight back, thus was denied the satisfaction of returning violence for violence's sake. She reveled in making me a target; she was the ultimate creator of all the abuse I suffered, in and out of the house. But despite who was to blame, I hated all the bullies to my very core. I wanted to hurt them. I dreamed of ways to make them go away for good. I could not fight back when the bullies came, but in the darkness, I dreamed.

———

In my dreams, I start a private graveyard on the property across the street from our house, filled with the bodies of all the bullies who have tormented me through the years. Here they lie, stacked like cordwood underground. I never dream of the act of killing them, just burying them, over and over again. They are covered in lime, wrapped in plastic, and tied with bailing twine. Into the ground they go, becoming desiccated and mummified over time. They will never hurt anyone again. I have seen to that. These dreams are becoming almost real to me. I truly fear I was going to get caught by the FBI for all of the bodies I had buried in that place. My grip on reality was slipping away every night as I lay in the dark. I never did become violent, but in the darkness, I dreamed.

———

My dreams helped me cope with the harsh reality of the hell I was in. They were never pleasant or pretty, but they got me through one day at a time. I could not get revenge in the waking world; I was not strong enough to fight or brave enough to walk away. So, every night in my dreams, I struck back proudly and violently. I fought in a way I couldn't fight when I was awake. I am, however, quite certain that I was hanging on a precipice of insanity in those final days in that house. These escapist dreams were at first a therapy to help me get by, but they had started to take on a stronger, darker appeal to me in the waking world. They appealed to me so much that I had started to daydream ways to do the deed and get away with it while I was awake.

I occasionally watch documentaries and TV shows about true crime and serial killers. I always marvel at how they list the building blocks of a serial killer. Here is the serial killer trinity: an abusive mother figure, violence (dehumanizing acts are just an everyday occurrence for them), and, of course, sexual abuse. My childhood could be used as a template for the profile of almost any serial killer. Still, I am missing some other characteristics that could be included here. I have never tortured another living thing, for instance. My childhood had the potential to create something wicked deep inside of me, and I feel very strongly that if I had stayed in that house, I would have started to act out on my dreams. By the time I hit fifteen, I had been forged into something Lucille did not foresee; I was becoming a monster myself, only a different kind of monster. I am so glad I got out of that house before I crossed that line. It was a line there would be no coming back from crossing.

— 30 —

LET ME VENT FOR A BIT HERE

Venting can be good for the soul. It lets you get out all your pain, anger, and frustrations. To speak your mind freely and to let it all hang out with no fear of recrimination is liberating. The simple act of talking things out can be cathartic. Venting allows you to express all your feelings in a safe way. Venting allows your mind to process and organize your thoughts, and this can be healing. Letting your frustrations out like this helps in so many ways. That being said, let the lambasting begin. Please allow me to bare my fangs and let my anger flow for a moment. I have earned that. I only do this with the hope of healing. Sharing my pain here might help ease my pain just a little more. With each telling, the pain fades a little bit more. So now, it is time for me to vent. Let the healing continue!

To be honest with you, most days, I don't even think about what happened to me as a child. In almost every conceivable way, I have moved on from it. What I went through made me much stronger than most of you, yet I am still more fragile than most in many ways. I was born a blank slate, a tabula rasa, the sum total of my life experience good and bad combined. Put on that slate all of the abuse I endured as a child. Then add all the good and bad things that have happened to me since Kitt's Tavern. Every one of these experiences make up who I am today. I would not change any of it, if I could. Today, I have three children and one stepdaughter, and I love them all dearly. I am married to a woman whom I deeply love. To undo my past would unravel my present. I choose to live in the now. What I have now is worth the price I paid. I was not grateful for the bill, but I paid it anyway.

Now, down to brass tacks: I still get angry when I think back on my childhood. In fact, right now I am mad as hell. What was done was unforgivable; there is no excuse for what happened. I have been told by counselors over the years to simply forgive. I was advised that if I let it go, and just forgave my parents, I would start to heal. To hell with that! I cannot forgive. In point of fact, I choose not to forgive. I refuse. If my refusal is blocking true healing, then so be it. Does this make me a bad person? I do not think so, but if anyone thinks it does, I can live with that. This is my life. It is my own personal choice to not forgive. What would the point of forgiving them be, anyway? My parents never believed they did anything wrong. Lucille erased us from her life. Forty-plus years ago, we stopped existing for her. In Lucille's psychotic point of view, removing us from her life was justified. We were not worthy of her love, time, or attention. How can I forgive someone who does not think they need forgiveness in the first place? In her mind, we are not even worthy of existence.

I sit here, happy in my exile. Despite all of your machinations, I am happy now, Lucille. You did not win, and I will not forgive.

— 31 —

FAMILY

Much to my surprise, and in direct denial of my twisted childhood programming, I am now happily married. I found my true love and soulmate. Christine is always willing to take me just as I am. She puts up with me and all of my many idiosyncrasies, even as all of the damage that was done to my psyche as a child still stands. Some pain never goes away, but it is amazing what you can learn to put aside. You can learn to live with anything; it just takes a bit of effort. There are days I still feel like a broken toy, like damaged goods. On these days, I battle against the innermost fears from my youth, yet I can now defeat them. And with each victory against the demons, the world seems a bit brighter, a bit less clouded over by the weight of my past.

I often wonder what Christine sees in me. Can she not tell how broken I am? Why would she be willing to share her life with me? I am happy that she sees me for what I am, not what I often feel. She does not see me as I frequently see myself, as a broken thing. I believe that I am an unattractive man, an indelible lesson from my youth. When

I look into a mirror, I see nothing of value. I remember that I am not worthy of anyone's love, another indelible lesson from my youth. Yet Christine and my kin vehemently disagree with these notions. At times, I am convinced I am a failed human being. Intellectually, I know that these feelings are wrong. With time and love, I have learned to strive against them whenever they rear their ugly head.

I have a good life. I have a wife who loves me. I have children who love me. I have a sister who loves me. So, for them and because of them, I can easily push away my feelings of inadequacy. In the act of pushing those feelings away, I deny the violence of my past any power it has over me. I have learned a very important lesson in life: even if something is written indelibly, that does not mean it cannot be painted over. You can start with a fresh canvas, a new lease on life, and paint yourself a new life over the pain.

Christine remains by my side, steadfast in her belief that I am worthy of love—yet I don't feel very lovable, on the bad days. I can be just a tad self-depreciating on the days my most troublesome memories come out to play. But a lifetime of experience has taught me that I am actually worthwhile. I know I am deserving of my place in the world.

I suppose we all have bad days, don't we? I have days where I feel I am a waste of space. I find that I am afraid, at times for no reason at all. On those days, I feel like an empty husk just holding back the tears. I start to fear that I have upset the people around me in my life. I quite often ask people if I have offended them. Call me paranoid if you must, but I see anger everywhere. Just like Pavlov's dogs salivating to the sound of a bell, the specter of my abusive conditioning still lingers. After all the years of being told I was a bad seed as justification for what I endured, I still salivate. The conditioning from so many years without approval, love, and acceptance left its scars. I cannot and will not deny that scars were left on my soul in my youth.

There is one thing I do deny every day. When those scars start to ache, and they often do, I deny them any power over me. I used to live every day as if I was walking on broken glass. That lifestyle was exhausting. I was always worried about what people around me were thinking of me. That has finally changed. I have people who I care for, and who care about me now. They help keep me in check, stopping my monsters at the door, blocking their path so that I do not let them in. I no longer sit docilely by, letting my demons dance upon the graveyard of my youth. I embrace the love and support of those around me in my life. I see in their eyes all the confirmation I need to banish the damage of my past for another day.

Death is the great diminisher of family ties. Beggars, bakers, and butchers all face the reaper in the end. Ultimately, we are all born with a death sentence that we cannot avoid. Death, with its inevitable acts of attrition, has taken so much from me. It has taken my birthmother, opening the door for Lucille to come into my life. It has taken my adoptive mother as well; I miss Nettie still. It has taken both of my fathers; I miss my adoptive father George, and with an accepted sense of confusion, I find I miss my biological father as well. Death took my brother before I ever got to know him, and it took my oldest sister through the horrible world of addiction. Each and every one of them passed away far too soon in my eyes, and each with a tragic story of their own they can no longer tell.

I have one family member left in this world. My sister, Lisa, is blood of my blood and is precious to me. In a perfect world, Lisa and I would share a deep bond of family love, but no—thanks to our shared violent pasts, we have an *unbreakable* bond. Our bond was forged during the relentless abuse of our youths, the abuse that prevented us from developing into normal, unbroken people. Yet, somehow, we survived, taking all the broken pieces left inside of us to make a mosaic out of them. Am I a perfect brother? Hell no, I am not even close to perfect in that respect. How could I be? I never learned how to be a sibling. But somehow, despite all the conditioning and abuse, we found each other and share a deep bond now.

My relationship with Lisa is complicated. I have so many emotional scars that make it very hard for me to speak with her. Almost every time I speak to Lisa, it opens up those old wounds and memories. Our conversation picks away at the scabs that cover my suppressed emotions. It's not Lisa's fault, really, nor is it mine. We both have a pattern of emotional wounds large enough to last several lifetimes. So, as a result of this, I often avoid talking to Lisa for months on end. I do this because I am afraid of the pain. I am so afraid of the memories.

I often wonder if the inflictors of our scars ever feel any regret. Do they sit back and feel that they did no wrong, that it was all justified? Lisa and I lost our innocence in that world. Yet we were the children, the broken toys who managed to survive and thrive in spite of it all. Broken we may be, but we are still survivors. I raise my glass—a toast to all the survivors. And here, now, is my toast for the inflictors of the pain: may the devil greet you at the door when you meet your end.

My children continue to be a great source of joy to me through the years. I was certain that I would never have children. The old adage of "learn one, do one, teach one" was broken by me. I had been schooled in violence, but I had no desire to pass that violence on to anyone else.

But how could I be something that I had never learned to be? I had asked myself—could I be a loving father? Oh, please…I get so angry over the smallest things. Sometimes it is a raging, violent, irrational anger that wants to explode from deep within. How could I bring a child into this world knowing I harbor so much anger inside of me? How could I not hurt a child, being so angry all the time? In my mind, I was terrified of becoming a father. How could I be a father after all the anger and violence I had seen in my own childhood? I was afraid I was my father's son. I was afraid that because of the way I had been so casually abused, that I would be an abuser too. I had been taught that violence and cruelty was part of parenting. I was afraid I would do the same things to a child of my own, maybe even worse. What I learned from my parents about raising a child was all about neglect, emotional abuse, starvation, and physical abuse. There was just enough normalcy tossed in. Suffice it to say, I was afraid to have a child of my own for one reason: I was afraid I would continue the cycle of abuse on them.

When I was twenty-five, my first wife and I brought our first child into the world. I found, very soon after that, I was nothing like my father. All I felt was love for this precious bundle of joy who had entered my life. Did I lose my temper with him? Sure, I did. Did I ever lash out in anger and beat or abuse him? No, I did not. Then, in the next few years, I had two little girls come into my life as well. During all this time, I never felt the need to strike, abuse, or to frighten my children into submission. I never tried to make them feel less than what they were. Did I spank my children? Yes, I did. But I learned I could always hit the diaper for a good sound effect rather than inflict pain. When they grew out of diapers, the spanking came to an end.

I eventually learned that young children can be reasoned with. Sometimes just saying the word "no" does not cover it; a child might need to know the reason why you are saying no. A simple explanation that they might get hurt, for example, is often enough. However, if they did not want to be reasoned with, a good-old-fashioned "time out" can work wonders. I never had to hurt them to teach that. I look back now and think about the fear I had of being violent with my own children. I can now see it was a false fear. As they have grown older, we have become more distant from each other, but I still love all my children as much as the first day the nurse put them in my arms to hold them for the very first time. My heart was torn asunder on each of those days, and only my children can hold it together. I even have a stepdaughter now. We have gone a few verbal rounds now and again, but I call it growing pains. And I care for her as much as if she were my own blood.

I want to take the opportunity here to deeply and genuinely apologize to all my children for my shortcomings. I did not abuse them, but I did become distant, emotionally. FaceTime makes up for the actual distance these days, so there is no excuse for it. Adversity is a trigger for me. Once I sense adversity coming into the picture, I stick my head into the sand like an ostrich. I avoid things that hurt in every way possible. My divorce from my first wife tore me apart. I am quite over it now and I have moved on from that pain, but it started a cycle within me of ignoring the pain caused by the split. Seeing my children brought it all back to me every time they came over for a visit. It wasn't their fault I did this; it was all my past coming back to haunt me. It was a basic defense mechanism that I learned as an abused child. I learned to ignore and avoid anything that caused me pain or discomfort, and my relationship with my children fell by the wayside for a while. It turns out I did not become the abuser to my children that I feared. But I have failed to keep up any kind of relationship with them because it stirs up feelings in me I want to avoid. I am supposed to be someone else, a better father. The gift of my childhood's abusive ministrations made me what I am today. It's the gift that keeps on giving. It's a gift you cannot give back. It's a gift that shows up at the worst possible moments, breaking me down a little bit more each time it rears its ugly head.

My life is good now. I am working to rebuild the bridges I have burned throughout my life. I am learning each day, learning to be happy with who I am. It is a war, but some battles are worth fighting. I know I have to stop thinking of myself as damaged, so I kick those dark thoughts to the curb when they show up. I have reached a point in my life where I can speak of what happened and it does not destroy me. It still hurts when it shows its ugly face, but now I have the tools and the emotional support to let it pass right through me. My life is not perfect, but I am happy. The past is always there, and I must always be vigilant of it trying to return, but like I have said before—some wars need to be fought, even if it is just waged within my own mind. My happiness is worth the strife.

Despite how bad my past sounds, I am happy with my life. I have had a good life, in spite of all that transpired when I was a child. I am content with my lot. After I got out of Kitt's Tavern I went to a new high school. New possibilities surrounded me. I was encouraged to learn all I could. I had new acquaintances. I had the love of my new guardians to support me. Mom (Mrs. Finch) and Dad (Mr. Finch) were always there for me, through thick or thin. Eventually, with all the support from those around me, I finished high school. It was good for me to actually complete something in my life. I learned to like the sense of accomplishment I got from a completed task.

After graduating high school, I joined the United States Marine Corps. I loved being a marine. I even loved boot camp at Parris Island, of all places. It was a land of blood, sweat, tears, and the sand flea. I was very good at what I did. I was good at taking orders. I loved the feeling of belonging. I loved the feeling that I was part of something bigger than me. I was able to travel the world. I got to see the sunrise over the ocean in the Land of the Rising Sun. I got to watch with wonder as rainstorms cut a path through the desert. I saw many places and met people I never would have met as a civilian. During my downtime, I would go to the enlisted club and have a couple beers to relax. Shooting pool with my fellow marines was one of my favorite pastimes. Playing pitch, backgammon, and spades with my fellow marines are some of my favorite recollections. I even had fun in the jungle during monsoon season, trekking through the mud and between the trees. I loved the desert; you could spend your entire night just trying to count all the stars in that beautifully clear Mojave sky. And I reveled in those tests of endurance. A twenty-kilometer march? Bring it on. I was up to it. My blisters were my badge of honor at the end of the day. I did not quit; I can march through the pain. I was well trained for that. The world was my oyster, and I collected every pearl I found along the way. After I left the Corps, I became a former marine; there are no ex-marines.

I lived with my father, Mr. Finch, for several years after the Corps, and one day, I met a young lady while I was at work. We started dating, eventually got married, and had three children together. Sadly, my first marriage did not stick; we ended up being divorced after just seven years. We had some good years, but we did not communicate well, and that one issue led to the demise of our life together. I do not regret those years; I have three wonderful children as a result of our pairing. Dale is my oldest child and son; I named him after my brother who passed on so many years ago. Victoria is my oldest daughter, and K'Ehleyr is my youngest daughter, all three of whom have been a great joy to me since the days they were born.

I met my current wife on Second Life. Yes, I met my wife in a computer-generated world. If someone had told me this tidbit twenty years ago, that I would meet someone online and eventually fall in love and marry them, I would have scoffed at them and laughed. But here's the funny part—not only did I meet her online, but I moved all the way to Australia, over nine-thousand miles away, to marry her. I was working in an eighties club online called Blackhearts. She walked in and said "hi." That's it, that's how it all started. With a single hello. God has a sense of humor, and how I met my wife proves this fact.

On Friday, July 13, 2012, Christine and I became husband and wife. My life in Australia with Christine is amazing. I got to hold a koala. I have petted a kangaroo. I honeymooned in the rainforest. I have yet to acquire a taste for rugby or cricket, but they are growing on me. Ten years after moving here, I am even adapting to the metric system. It never gets cold, here in the tropics. I miss snow, especially around Christmas. Do I still fear the dark? Yes, but I am in control and can flick on a light to make the darkness go away whenever I want to. Does my past still come back to haunt me? Yes, it does, but I have the love of those around me to help make it go away.

My mind still boggles over how I ended up so far from the place of my birth. But here I am. I am happy, I am content, I am loved. Who knew?

— 32 —

FINAL THOUGHTS

Time. We are all granted a very limited amount of time in this world. We are all born with an expiration date, with no foreknowledge of what our final act will be.

I will put those morbid thoughts aside, however, and get to the point. Time was a deciding factor for me when choosing to tell this story. How much time do I have left on this planet to pass on this narrative of my youth? So many horrible things happen to people in this world. In this social media society we live in, we cannot avoid being exposed to stories from the darker side of life. This world can be abusive and harsh, leaving victims helpless in its wake. Based on my background and experiences, I believe that I can help the victims of these despicable acts in some way. Maybe, just maybe, I can pass on a kernel of knowledge to a new generation of victims out there. My lifetime of experience, of learning how to cope with unspeakable trauma, is a message worth delivering. I think my words matter. I believe I can make a difference. Maybe, in some way, I can help ease someone's pain. If this book helps just one shattered person become whole again, I will be content. This endeavor will have been worth the effort and pain of its creation.

Is it conceit to be proud that I lived through hell and came out stronger for it? I am proud of who I now am today, I know that. Is it conceited to think that I learned something that can help others in the very act of surviving? No, it is not. I walked the walk and now I can talk the talk with confidence and hard-earned knowledge. I am now in my mid-fifties. How much time do I have left? Ever since I got away from Kitt's Tavern I knew I had a story to tell. I have always wanted to write a book detailing what happened in that house. I am older and wiser now, and time's a-wasting. The time has come for me to step up and finally tell the twisted tale of my violent childhood. It is time to share this story with the world.

Shame. The main obstruction to writing this narrative can be attributed to this one word. In the telling of my story, I knew I would have to bare my soul and tell all. I would have to reveal all my most humiliating and embarrassing moments to the world, letting out all my dirty, disgusting, nasty secrets for all to hear. I was abused for years in that house. I allowed all of it to happen and had no choice in the matter. I was a victim, pure and simple. I know that now. But a victim can still feel deep and powerful shame for what was done to them. I could never have fought back in that house, yet I was ashamed that I never tried. The knowledge and acceptance of where the blame lies, of whom is at fault, does not make the shame magically go away. Over time, I learned to cope with my memories and nightmares, but it has never been the shame. I don't want sympathy about what happened to me—it is my past; sympathy cannot undo what was done to me. Sympathy only makes me feel like a victim all over again and shames me more. I also knew that if I excluded anything important from this narrative, I would deeply regret it. So, because I was not yet willing to tell the whole story, I put off writing this book.

I am emotionally strong enough now to say I was horribly abused. I did not choose for it to happen. Why should I feel shame for actions that were done to me? I had no choice; I was a child. For years, I carried so much shame. I could only talk about it in rooms where medical privilege applied. Lisa and I speak of it often, just trying to understand the inexplicability of it all. To paraphrase the words of Malcolm X, we didn't land on Kitt's Tavern; Kitt's Tavern landed on us. What was done to us was unforgivable. But here's the thing: forgiveness was never part of the equation. The true lesson was learning how to live with the damage done to us and still thrive. Finally, I am ready. I do not care what people think of me anymore. It is time to let the past run free.

Here, there be monsters. The world is full of monsters. The devil wears blue jeans. They walk amongst us every day. The damage they do is unquantifiable. It is unquantifiable because so many victims refuse to speak. They do not speak of the violent acts that have been done to them because of the shame they carry. It is emotionally devastating to speak about the pain that has burrowed itself so deep into one's soul.

I do have one suggestion for all the silent victims out there: please, jump up and shout, "This happened to me! The monsters are real!" I find that letting the story out is a healing balm that gets better with every repetition. Speak to someone who is safe for you in your situation. It could be family, clergy, councilors, friends, or anyone you feel comfortable with. Tell them everything. Hold nothing back; half measures do not work. They say confession is good for the soul. Confessing that you are a victim is cathartic, because you eventually realize you have nothing to confess. Do this according to your comfort level, of course. And you need to wholeheartedly trust any person you speak to.

Trust. Trust is an issue for victims of abuse. I am aware of this concept quite intimately. If you cannot speak to someone about it, there are other options. Write it in a journal and let your journal be your confessor. Poetry, lyrics, painting, meditating, long showers, mindfulness, working out, running, walking...all these and more can help you cope and get the pain and frustrations out of your mind and into the open. Someday, you might start trusting enough to share with someone who has a truly sympathetic ear. But until then, learn to cope to your heart's content. Let out the inner flames caused by the abuse. Do not let them burn you up on the inside. Don't become a husk of what you used to be.

I am not a mental health worker. I do not pretend to be a professional helper. What I have learned, I have learned the hard way, through the school of hard knocks. It is amazing what you can live through, and it is just as amazing what you can learn to live with. Surviving is just the first step in a lifetime of steps toward recovery. I know, I have walked that path. And I am only human, so I have stumbled so many times along the way. I think about how I declined so much help on my personal path for so long. The best move that I made was to walk away. I don't do confrontation. I eventually found my answers. I got help. I found my way back to a fulfilling life. But God, was it a bumpy road with so many casualties along the way. Please don't do as I did at the start of all this. Denial was a wonderfully destructive thing for me, but denial was so unproductive in the end. Don't be like I was. Seek help at the beginning. Don't run away from the pain. Pain is nature's way of telling you something is wrong. Pain tells you that you need repair. Heed pain's warning. Let someone in to help you heal.

There is no magic pill you can take to make this go away. There is no quick fix. But there is healing, in time. Just let people into your life to help you face your pain. Do the nightmares ever stop? I do not know yet. For me, they still creep in from time to time. But I can tell you they do get better over time. What I am saying is, I am still fighting my battles. But they have become easier to win with treatment, effort, time, and understanding.

True healing takes time. Forty years later, the healing process is still happening for me. Life plods on. Some wounds never truly heal, but we learn to slap a bandage on them and carry on. But it is what you do with those old wounds that matters most. I choose to live life with a sense of joy and wonder. I choose to see the beauty in the world around me. I love this life I have now, and I would choose no other path than the one that took me here today. Every day I get to choose what kind of person I want to be. I will not be a victim; in fact, I deny that I am victim anymore. I am a survivor. I survived.

I ask anyone who reads these words I have written to listen to one final piece of advice from me. Pain is fleeting, and it can be defeated. Keep your chin up and know things will get better over time. It might not look that way right now, but it does get better. I am living evidence of that. Do not give power to your pain; let it go. Become a survivor.

Live.

And Love.

POSTSCRIPT

As I have mentioned, I never really knew my sister Lori; she was larger than life to me when I was very young and had run away from home before I ever got to know her. I tried so hard to help her with her addictions, but nothing seemed to help. Just the sweet oblivion of her next fix was enough, in her world, to make the memories of the monsters go away. One of the greatest disappointments in my life was to fail in my attempts to help her heal.

I wrote a short story about my earliest memory of violence in the house and sent it to her. She replied with several Facebook messages, one of which I saw and one message that I did not see until after she died. I guess I just missed it, somehow. I was scrolling back through her messages not too long after Lori's death and I found the message from her that I had missed. It turned my blood cold.

I am posting the two messages below. I will forever wish I had a chance to speak to her about what happened to us in that house. (The following was edited for spelling and punctuation only.)

> I am really happy to hear from you. I think now maybe it may have been the time when I was in high school, and we had double sessions and I went in the afternoon. I went to school and after school I

ran away to Aunt Phyllis and Uncle Tom's house, and Dad (so called Dad) came over and got me and threatened he would call the cops on me if I ever ran away again. He scared the living shit out of me to where I believed him. But other than that, I cannot think of how or when the events might have fallen. I did end up running away again at the age of seventeen. I went from feeling and being treated like a dog to being a human being who knew how it felt to bathe, eat, and be treated like I was normal. I would say [Lucille] had this way about her to where outsiders saw the picture that she wanted. She did not seem to care that a few people here and there saw through her and what she really was. How old where you when Mr. and Mrs. Finch took you in? I do not recall; I am sure it could not have been soon enough. I wish I had been there for you when you were growing up, part of me blames myself for what happened to you and Lisa. But the reality that I know now is that I could not have changed what they did. I only know that in time they will have to somehow pay for their wrongdoings. I must sign off now, I will keep you and Christine in my prayers. Tell her I said hello.

Love Lori

———

David, I really miss you, it has been years, but to get to the subject, I keep reading about something you wrote about your past, our past lovely family life (ha). And I say that with my heart wrenching. I can only imagine what they did to you and Lisa after I left. I only know that after I left I finally felt like a real human, not like a dog anymore. I was no longer being abused in any way a girl can be abused, and I mean any way. I cannot fathom how a father in his right frame of mind could do that to his own daughter. But the lousy bastard did it. There is a lot of hatred which is never spoken about, not even with a counselor. I suppose I should do that, but I am afraid it will unleash some of this untreated anger I have. So enough of me...sorry I went off on an "oh it's all about me" tangent. So how are you doing? You will have to send me some more of your writing if you don't mind sharing it with me. Does it help to write about it? So how is married life and living in Australia? You lucky duck it must be beautiful there compared to here. Tell Christine I said hello. It was nice to get a message back from her about a week ago. It meant a lot to me, please tell her that. I am at the Dr's, so I hope you get this message.

Love Lori

AFTERWORD

After editing dozens of books on a wide variety of topics, it is a surreal feeling to edit one in which I find myself to be a character. Not by name, of course, just by association.

I am two years older than David, and one year younger than his sister Lisa. My family lived less than a mile up the road from Kitt's Tavern, and my pick-up was before theirs along the winding Weaver Hill Road bus route. Every morning, I watched them all board the bus—Michael and Monique first, bouncing and bright-eyed as they sprinted for the back seats to sit with the cool kids, followed by David and Lisa looking gray and tattered with dead eyes, slogging along the best they could, hoping someone would be charitable enough to let them sit next to them. Each morning, like many of the riders, I hoped I wouldn't be the unlucky one.

I looked down upon them like every other kid did. I am not proud of that. I don't think I every bullied either of them, as it was not in my nature, but I am embarrassed to admit that I probably would have in the right situation. I was grateful for people like David and Lisa to distract the bullies away from me as I struggled with my own immaturity, fears, and childhood anxiety.

I remember being driven to school one morning by my parents (maybe I missed the bus that day) and we saw Lisa marching up the breakdown lane of Nooseneck Hill Road on her lonely, four-mile trek to school. We did not stop, but no one else did, either.

I remember knocking on the door of Kitt's Tavern one Halloween night. Dale answered, then brought my brother and me down to the entrance of the cellar, where he offered us potatoes and onions for our goody bags. I believe he thought he was being funny—and in another reality, he might have been—but the longer we stood in the entryway to the cellar, the more uneasy I felt. The darkness behind him that reached into the depths of the cellar looked cold and cavernous, like you'd expect to see beneath a haunted house. In that moment in my mind, Dale was a sentinel at the gates of Hell. This wasn't that fun kind of Halloween frightfulness, either. Even at ten years old, my Spidey-sense told me there was something terrible down there. I think our father sensed it too, and I was grateful when he interrupted and pulled us out of there when he did.

I remember playing baseball against David in the senior league. I recall pitching a no-hitter at the start of the last inning when he came to the plate. He was always an easy out, and I was clinging to a one-run lead. I remember my first pitch hitting him in the ribs and the roar of laughter that erupted from their bench as it happened. I think his teammates enjoyed seeing him doubled over in pain as much as they enjoyed getting a free baserunner in a close game. I remember being furious at myself for letting the team's worst player reach base, and then for letting that mistake rattle me into an eventual 2–1 loss.

And I remember two players one day getting into a fistfight at third base, and Dale, their coach, grabbing them by their shirts to pull them apart. I remember the mother of one of the boys charging across the field at full speed to dive into the fracas, not to chastise her own son for being a shit, but to pound on Dale. Like the rest of us, she knew all the horror stories, and in her mind, Dale was the chief perpetrator. Having him place his abusive hands upon her son for any reason was simply too much to bear.

After I aged out of the baseball league as a player, I returned to coach with my dad for my younger brother's team and earn a few bucks as the league's official scorekeeper. While I was scoring, Lucille would drag her lawn chair up next to mine and we would chat about the game. She was always pleasant and happy, but there was an innate oddness about her that I find difficult to explain even now. For some reason, she liked me; she thought I would be the perfect match for Monique, and she often urged me to ask her out. But I had zero interest. I heard the rumors. I knew the stories, like everyone else did. As hard as Lucille tried to maintain appearances and keep the evil under wraps, in the end, the joke was on her—*we all knew*.

And I remember Mr. Finch—the most terrifying man I ever met when I was ten years old. His natural presence, his steely eyes, and his booming voice were a natural for middle school leadership. (Think of him as an angry Joaquin Phoenix.) And I remember him returning to the field one evening with David when he was about sixteen years old to watch a game. I had a brief conversation with Mr. Finch that night and was amazed he even remembered me as the quiet, nearly invisible kid I once had been. I was instantly struck by the man's friendliness, humor, and grace. I deeply regret not having the opportunity to get to know George Finch better. There was so much to admire. And as for David, I recall being taken back by how unusual he looked that night. This David was somehow different from the decrepit version I remembered from the school bus years earlier. It took me a while to realize why. It was because he was smiling.

So, the years rolled by. I went to college, got married, had kids, developed a career, wrote a few books, and started a publishing company. And through those years, I told my family all about my exploits growing up in West Greenwich as a kid, and even included a few tales of that sad, strange family that lived in the spectacular, beautifully restored house on the corner.

And then, last year, out of the blue, I received an unexpected message from David. He was working on a manuscript about his childhood and saw somewhere on social media that I might be able to help him.

The first question David asked was, "Do you remember me?"

There are a few heroes in this story, but there could have been so many more. To me, the greatest tragedy here is how many people knew what was happening but made a conscious decision to look away. You would be within your rights to point fingers at the family members, or the police, or the state, or teachers, or coaches, and so many others, but that's too easy. We *all* had the chance to be heroes, but we all turned our backs to the neglect and abuse that we all knew was happening. In my opinion, the greatest tragedy here is that in the darkest moments, the saga of the Harter children lived openly on the lips and tongues of everyone who came into contact with them.

In the end, we were the monsters.

Steven R. Porter, Publisher
Stillwater River Publications

ABOUT THE AUTHOR

David lives in Far North Queensland with his wife Christine and their cats.
www.instagram.com/david_l_h_finch/

www.ingramcontent.com/pod-product-compliance
Lightning Source LLC
Chambersburg PA
CBHW071113160426
43196CB00013B/2555